Royal Horticultural Society

# RHS Allotment
# JOURNAL

RHS Allotment Journal

First published in Great Britain in 2010 by Mitchell Beazley,
an imprint of Octopus Publishing Group Ltd, in association
with The Royal Horticultural Society.

Endeavour House, 189 Shaftesbury Avenue, London WC2H 8JY
**www.octopusbooks.co.uk**

An Hachette UK Company
www.hachette.co.uk

The Royal Horticultural Society is the UK's leading gardening charity dedicated to
advancing horticulture and promoting good gardening. Its charitable work includes
providing expert advice and information, training the next generation of gardeners,
creating hands-on opportunities for children to grow plants, and conducting research
into plants, pests, and environmental issues affecting gardeners. For more information
visit www.rhs.org.uk or call 0845 130 4646.

ISBN: 978 1 84533 559 5

A CIP record for this book is available from the British Library.

Set in Granjon Vietnamese, Interstate and Caecilia.

Printed and bound in China.

**Commissioning Editor**  Helen Griffin
**General Editor**  Geoff Hodge
**Senior Editor**  Leanne Bryan
**Copy-editor**  Lynn Bresler
**Proofreader**  Alexandra Stetter
**Indexer**  Diana Lecore
**Art Director**  Pene Parker
**Deputy Art Director**  Yasia Williams-Leedham
**Designer**  Mark Kan
**Picture Research Manager**  Giulia Hetherington
**Production Controller**  Susan Meldrum

**RHS Publisher**  Susannah Charlton
**RHS Commissioning Editor**  Rae Spencer-Jones

Royal Horticultural Society

# RHS Allotment
# JOURNAL

MITCHELL BEAZLEY

# Contents

# JANUARY

*Make a start on digging over the soil to get it ready for planting – especially important on heavy clay soils.*

# This month...

The start of the year is usually renowned for freezing weather and driving rain – not appealing conditions to spend time on the allotment – but there's still plenty you can do.

Luckily, much of it can be done in the warm inside. There are seeds and plants to order, seedtrays, pots, cloches and frames to clean and even a bit of early indoor sowing – such as onions, leeks and some brassicas. Indoor sowings will need warmth, so do it in a heated propagator or on a warm, sunny windowsill.

Outside, you can keep warm by starting – or finishing – digging over the soil to get it ready for sowing. This is particularly important on heavy clay soils, providing they're not waterlogged; light, sandy soils are best left until early spring. While you're digging, incorporate home-made garden compost or manure into soil to be used for potatoes and other heavy feeders.

Established freestanding apple and pear trees are pruned this month, but only do it if necessary. Young trees and trees that are cropping well are often best left well alone, apart from removing dead, diseased or other unwanted growth. There are other fruits that need pruning now too, including grapevines and currants.

Out on the allotment, there should be plenty of crops for harvesting: leeks, many brassicas and parsnips, sweetened by a touch of frost, will all be ready for the kitchen. And, of course, stores of onions, potatoes and apples can all be used, together with any excess summer crops sitting in the freezer.

If you're missing out on salads, there are some hardier winter salad crops that can be sown in the glasshouse and even sprouting seeds on a windowsill. As an organised plotholder you'll never go hungry.

# Top veg jobs

- Start drawing up your plans for this year's vegetable cropping and order seeds and other planting material – including onion sets and seed potatoes. When seeds arrive, make a month-by-month seed-sowing organiser and store the seeds in cool, dry conditions.

- Some indoor sowings can be made, but windowsills are rather dark and seedlings suffer if grown on them for prolonged periods. Glasshouses offer better conditions, but some heating will be needed to provide a minimum temperature of 7–10°C (45–50°F) for most crops.

- Sow broad beans, Brussels sprouts, early summer cabbage, calabrese, cauliflowers, leeks, onions, peas, radishes, shallots, spinach and turnips.

- Plant out young broad bean and winter lettuce plants. They will need cloche or fleece protection.

- Plant shallots and garlic in mild areas with well drained soil. They can be planted in modules under cover if conditions aren't right outside.

- Radishes, mustard, cress, winter lettuce and other salads can be sown in growing bags in a glasshouse or on a windowsill.

- Make a trench where you're going to grow peas and beans, leeks and celery and fill it with kitchen vegetable waste, torn up newspaper, cardboard, compost and anything similar. This will help hold moisture in the summer and so produce bumper crops.

- As you harvest winter crops, clear away any remaining vegetation and put it on the compost heap or, if it is suffering from severe disease, dispose of it. Crop and other plant debris left lying around becomes a home and breeding place for pests and diseases.

## ALLOTMENT REMINDERS

✔ Spring cabbages can be used as winter greens if they are large enough.

✔ Plant Jerusalem artichoke tubers.

✔ Regularly check stored crops and remove rotting and mouldy ones.

✔ Protect brassica crops from pigeons or the birds will tear them to shreds.

✔ Buy in sufficient seedtrays, pots, canes, string, stakes and netting, as well as fertiliser, compost and pesticides.

## VEG OF THE MONTH – LEEKS

A stalwart winter vegetable, leeks are easy to grow. By sowing different varieties at different times you can have crops available from autumn to spring.

**Leek tips:** Sow thinly 1cm (½in) deep in rows 15cm (6in) apart in a seedbed from mid- to late spring.

- For a late summer to autumn crop, sow indoors in seedtrays with warmth from mid- to late winter. Transplant the seedlings to cell trays and plant outside in mid-spring.

- Transplant to their final positions when they are about 15–20cm (6–8in) high and the thickness of a pencil. Water well before lifting. Make 5cm (2in) wide, 15cm (6in) deep holes with a dibber 15cm (6in) apart and drop a plant into each. Fill the hole with water to settle the roots.

**"From plot to plate in a matter of minutes – you really can't beat the freshness of home-grown fruit and veg"**

# Vichyssoise

**Serves 6**

Takes 1 hour, plus chilling

**Ingredients**

1kg (2lb 4oz) leeks

50g (1¾oz) butter

1 onion, chopped

1 litre (1¾ pints) vegetable stock

pinch of grated nutmeg

750g (1lb 10oz) old potatoes, diced

600ml (1 pint) milk

300ml (½ pint) single cream

150ml (¼ pint) double cream

salt and white pepper

2 tbsp snipped chives, to garnish

**1** Slice off the green tops of the leeks and set them aside for use in another recipe. Thinly slice the white parts of the leeks.

**2** Melt the butter in a large, heavy-based saucepan. Add the leeks and onion and cook over a moderate heat for 5 minutes or until softened but not coloured.

**3** Add the stock, nutmeg and potatoes and season to taste with salt and pepper. Bring to the boil. Reduce the heat, partially cover the pan and simmer for 25 minutes. Pour in the milk and simmer for 5–8 minutes. Leave to cool slightly.

**4** Put the soup in a food processor or blender and blend, in batches if necessary, until smooth, then rub it through a sieve into a bowl. Add the single cream, stir well and cover closely.

**5** Chill the soup in the refrigerator for at least 3 hours. Just before serving, swirl in the double cream, then taste and adjust the seasoning if necessary. Serve the soup in chilled bowls, garnishing each portion with a generous sprinkling of snipped chives.

# Top fruit jobs

• January is a great month to plant just about any new fruit. Always check rootstocks and pollination groups before ordering fruit trees. If the planting site isn't ready when plants arrive, heel in bare-root ones in the ground, covering the roots with soil. Leave containerised ones in a sheltered position and water the compost when needed to prevent it drying out.

• After planting, mulch the soil around fruit with a 5–7.5cm (2–3in) thick layer of organic matter to prevent weeds growing and maintain soil moisture levels during summer.

• There are plenty of pruning jobs to get on with. Start or continue the winter pruning of established, freestanding apple and pear trees. Make sure you have a plan of attack and don't just prune for the sake of it.

• Currants and gooseberries can be pruned now. Start by thinning out very old, very thin and diseased growth.

• Prune red and white currants and gooseberries by cutting back main branches by half to three quarters, and sideshoots on these branches to one to three buds from their base.

• For black currants, cut back up to one third to a half of all the older branches to their base to give plenty of room for young, vigorous growth.

• Lift and divide old, unproductive crowns of rhubarb and replant in well-prepared soil with plenty of added well-rotted manure or similar bulky organic matter.

• Place a large bucket, dustbin or forcing jar over a rhubarb crown to encourage the fresh, pink shoots to form. Some manure or straw and poultry manure pellets placed over the soil first will create extra warmth to speed up forcing.

• Rabbits, deer and squirrels will gnaw away at bark. Protect plants by wrapping their stems in plastic tree protectors.

• Protect fan-trained peaches and nectarines from peach leaf curl with a 'tent' of plastic sheeting attached to the top of the supporting

*Mulch around the base of fruit trees with lots of well-rotted manure or similar organic material.*

structure. Roll this down to soil level about 45cm (18in) away from the base of the tree and secure.

## Pruning tools

Ensure your cutting tools are sharp and clean. **Secateurs** are the most important pruning tool. Bypass secateurs give the best cuts.

**Loppers** are long-handled secateurs with a wider mouth to cut thicker branches; the long handles provide extra leverage.

**Tree loppers** (long-handled secateurs) are perfect for getting at high branches.

Use a **pruning saw** for all thick branches that secateurs or loppers can't cope with.

A **pruning knife** is useful for cutting back soft growth and paring the bark smooth after removing larger branches.

## ALLOTMENT REMINDERS

✔ Remove and destroy mummified apples, pears and plums affected with brown rot to prevent the disease from spreading.

✔ Place cloches over strawberry plants for an early crop.

✔ It is essential to prune grapevines while they're dormant.

"The answer DOES lie in the soil – get to know yours if you want the best results"

# Groundwork

Before you can turn a new allotment plot into a productive fruit and veg production unit, you'll probably need to do some basic groundwork.

## Clearing weeds

This will probably be the initial thing to consider.

• Covering the soil with a black plastic sheet for a few months or even a growing season, or treating with a glyphosate-based weedkiller, will bring the ground into a workable condition quickly.

• After clearing, if possible destroy all vegetation by burning (be sensitive to other plotholders and follow any site rules) or, better, by composting.

• Dig over the soil bit by bit, getting rid of any weed roots as you go, working to the depth of a spade's blade. Deeper digging is not essential.

• If there are no perennial weed roots, or if you have killed them with weedkiller, hire or borrow a cultivator to break up the soil. Note, though, that a cultivator chops weed roots into fine pieces making any remaining weeds even worse, and if used in the wet it can ruin the soil structure.

*Below Test the pH level of the soil regularly.*
*Right Use a spade to bury annual weeds, organic matter and debris, then leave a level surface.*

## Check the soil structure

Dig a pit about 60cm (24in) deep. You should see about 25cm (10in) depth of dark topsoil, without hard, compressed zones that plant roots cannot penetrate.

• To check that the underlying subsoil is not rock hard but will allow water to drain, fill the pit with water, cover to keep out rain, and leave overnight. If the water is gone by morning all is well; if not, drainage may be a problem.

• If topsoil or good subsoil are lacking, serious soil improvement will be needed.

• Poor drainage is often best overcome by growing in raised beds.

## Soil testing

Plants need nutrients to grow, especially nitrogen, phosphorus, potassium and magnesium.

• A laboratory soil test is well worth investing in. It will tell you soil pH (whether it is acid or alkaline) and how much phosphorus, potassium and magnesium it contains. This allows you to choose the right fertiliser to use.

• If the soil is acid, it will need lime to 'sweeten' it. Fruit likes acid soil, but for most vegetables (except potatoes) alkaline conditions are better and will reduce diseases, especially club root.

# Family allotments

*Allotments give children the opportunity to get close to soil, plants and insects.*

For families, the allotment is a place to have fun and exercise in the fresh air, learn about plants and wildlife and meet friends to play with. Just keep to a few basic rules so that it is clear where and where not to tread, what and what not to pick, and so on, and family life on the allotment really can be a pleasure for everyone.

A family allotment should be managed just as any other allotment, but with special thought in a few specific areas. Young children usually have a short attention span, so visits to the plot are best kept to frequent short-and-sweet trips to maintain interest. Or have lunch there, maybe with a camping stove so that you can cook produce immediately – there's nothing to beat freshly barbecued sweet corn.

Ensure you all know what you want to do each visit, so that you're raring to go on arrival. Exercise caution and be safe. Make sure that potentially dangerous chemicals are out of reach, be vigilant about physical dangers (such as tools left on paths as a tripping hazard), ensure all stakes and canes are topped off to save eyes and be aware of water containers that could present a drowning danger.

Some crops might need a little careful explanation: gooseberries can be very thorny and sharp;

rhubarb leaves can't be eaten, even though they look similar to chard; and just because we eat mangetout peas, it doesn't mean you can eat sweet peas.

## What to grow with a family

Choose allotment crops that tick at least one of the following boxes: quick results (radishes or rocket); minimal work (rhubarb); popular with children (strawberries); exciting to harvest (potatoes); easy or fun to harvest (peas); likely to succeed (courgettes).

• Let the children help choose what to grow.

• Give each child a patch of ground, so they get to choose what to do with it.

• Show them how to sow in rows, patterns and letters to spell their name.

• It's their space, but make sure that they are involved with the whole plot.

## Keeping children occupied

Apart from sowing and harvesting, there are other ways to engage your children.

• Most youngsters love getting their hands dirty and will want to play with the soil. Ask them to clear a defined (and small) patch of ground of weeds with a trowel.

• Give them a spray pump full of water, although it may not be just the plants that get wet.

• Let them make a bird scarer out of old CDs strung up, or cans on sticks.

• Sometimes, children will relish a challenge that we don't. Ask them to find and dispose of all the cabbage white caterpillars from the brassicas, or slugs and snails.

*Harvesting strawberries is instantly gratifying – as long as you have grown enough.*

# FEBRUARY

1. Finish pruning apple and pear trees.   2. Make a start on indoor seed sowing.
3. Rhubarb will be ready to crop if you've protected the crown.   4. Polythene will warm the soil and protect early crops.

# This month...

February is often colder than January, but the indoor jobs you started last month can be completed in the warm if you didn't get a chance to finish them.

At this time of year there is an almost irresistible urge to start sowing seeds outside and planting out, but be patien. Unless your soil is very well drained and you live in a sheltered, mild district, it is far better to wait until spring. Most vegetable seeds won't germinate until the soil temperature reaches 7°C (45°F) and if sown in cold soil will just rot. Sowings made in spring, in better conditions, will catch up with those sown now and usually produce better, stronger plants.

But you can get ready for an early start outside by covering the soil with clear polythene. This warms up the soil, protects it from getting too soggy and encourages weeds to germinate, so they can then be dealt with before sowing to produce a 'weed-free' bed.

You can sow seeds inside with heat if you can provide the right conditions. In the fruit garden you'll need to protect the blossom of early-flowering apricots, peaches and nectarines from frost damage by covering with fleece.

You need to finish apple and pear pruning as soon as possible and it is a good idea to check on fruit cages, especially the netting, replacing it if it has become damaged. At this time of year, birds, especially bullfinches, may peck at developing fruit buds, reducing the summer yield.

And if you were very clever and thought ahead and protected a crown of rhubarb, you might be able to tuck in to the first, tasty sticks.

# Top veg jobs

• If you've kept seeds from previous years, check them to ensure they're still worth sowing. Small seeds can be given a germination test: place 20 on moist kitchen paper and put somewhere warm. After about seven days, check for germination. If the germination rate is less than 50 per cent (10 seeds germinate) they may not be worth keeping.

• It is sometimes better to buy young vegetable plants or seedlings rather than take the time, trouble, effort and cost of raising your own from seed – for instance grafted vegetables. Check catalogues and place orders now, as they can be in short supply by spring.

• From the middle of the month onward you can start to sow seeds of tomatoes, peppers, aubergines and cucumbers for plants to grow in a glasshouse. Sow the seeds in small pots of good compost and germinate in a heated propagator or warm room at 21–24°C (70–75°F).

• If you want plants for growing outside or can't provide the right temperatures and conditions, delay sowing until March.

• Starting peas under cover gives them a head start. For an alternative method for indoor sowing, sow peas in a glasshouse in lengths of guttering. Drill drainage holes in the bottom and fill with good compost. When ready for planting out, the whole row can be gently pushed out of the guttering.

• Chit seed potatoes, as this generally produces a bigger, better crop – especially early potato varieties. Chitting means starting the seed tubers into growth to produce strong young shoots before planting them out.

• Stand the seed potatoes in trays or egg boxes with the 'rose' end (the end with the most eyes or buds) uppermost. Keep somewhere cool, light and frost-free. The tubers will be ready to plant out in late March and throughout April.

---

## ALLOTMENT REMINDERS

✔ All the January jobs can still be carried out in February.

✔ Clean out and wash seedtrays, pots and other containers ready for seed sowing.

---

## VEG OF THE MONTH – CABBAGE

With planning it's possible to pick fresh cabbages every day of the year. Although traditionally green, there are also red or purple cabbages and a range of shapes.

**Cabbage tips:** Sow thinly 1cm (½in) deep in rows 15cm (6in) apart in a seedbed. Sow little and often to ensure a succession of crops. Thin seedlings to 7.5cm (3in) apart.

• Sow summer cabbage from late winter to spring (with protection or indoors); winter cabbage from late spring to early summer; spring cabbage in summer.

• Plant out the young plants when they are ready, 30–45cm (12–18in) apart. Plant spring cabbages 10cm (4in) apart in rows 30cm (1ft) apart; thin these to 30cm (1ft) apart in winter and use them as spring greens.

**"**Unlike buying fruit and veg, growing your own allows you to choose varieties that have the best taste**"**

# Borscht with soured cream & chives

**Serves 6**

Takes 1 hour 25 minutes

**Ingredients**

750g (1lb 10oz) raw beetroot, washed

1 carrot, peeled and grated

1 onion, grated

2 garlic cloves, crushed

1.5 litres (2¾ pints) vegetable stock

4 tbsp lemon juice

2 tbsp sugar

1 large cooked beetroot

salt and pepper

**To garnish**

150ml (¼ pint) soured cream

1 tsp snipped chives

**1** Scrape young beetroot or peel older ones, then coarsely grate the raw beetroot flesh into a large saucepan.

**2** Add the carrot, onion, garlic, vegetable stock, lemon juice and sugar and season to taste with salt and pepper. Bring to the boil, reduce the heat, cover the pan and simmer for 45 minutes.

**3** Meanwhile, cut the whole cooked beetroot into matchsticks about 3.5cm (1½in) long. Cover and chill until needed.

**4** When the soup vegetables are tender, strain the contents of the pan through a muslin-lined sieve. Discard the vegetables.

**5** Return the soup to the rinsed pan with the beetroot matchsticks. Bring the soup gently to the boil, then simmer for a few minutes to warm the beetroot through.

**6** Season the soup to taste with salt and pepper, then ladle it into warm bowls and serve with a spoonful of soured cream and garnished with snipped chives.

# Top fruit jobs

*Autumn raspberries should be cut back to ground level in late winter.*

• Apply a general-purpose balanced fertiliser to all fruit. Fertiliser should be applied over the whole root area – roughly equivalent to the spread of the branches. Adding a potassium-rich feed can also be beneficial, especially for heavy-cropping fruits and those that didn't crop well last year.

• Mulch all fruit crops with well-rotted manure or garden compost after feeding.

• Prune autumn-fruiting raspberries (not summer-fruiting or recently planted Primocanes), cutting down the canes to the ground before mulching with well-rotted manure or compost and topdressing with fertiliser. Summer raspberries can be cut back to one or two buds above the top of their supporting wires if they've grown too tall.

• For an early crop of strawberries, place cloches or fleece over plants. Lift the cover during warm days when plants are in flower, to give pollinating insects access to the flowers for pollination. High-potassium feeds (such as tomato fertiliser) will also help encourage flowers and fruit.

• Hand-pollinate flowers of apricots, peaches and nectarines if insects are scarce. A small, soft paintbrush or a rabbit's tail are the best tools for transferring the pollen from flower to flower.

## ALLOTMENT REMINDERS

✔ Last chance to plant bare-root fruit trees and bushes – this needs to be completed by the end of the month.

✔ Finish all winter pruning.

✔ Force rhubarb clumps for an early crop.

## FRUIT OF THE MONTH – APPLES

Apples are not only versatile in the kitchen, they're adaptable on the allotment, where they lend themselves to shapes including fans, espaliers and cordons. They are by far the easiest tree fruit to grow and can be cultivated in the smallest of spaces thanks to dwarfing rootstocks.

**Apple tips:** When choosing which apples to grow, try sourcing more unusual varieties that are local to your area. Chances are they'll be more suited to the soils and climate on your plot.

Apple trees are grafted onto a rootstock to control height.

M27: Extremely dwarfing, for growing trees up to 1.8m (6ft).

M9: Very dwarfing, for trees grown in pots or producing a freestanding tree of 2–2.5m (6½–8ft).

M26: Semi-dwarfing, the best for pots, cordons and espaliers.

# February

"Early, forced rhubarb
is the first pink jewel
to harvest from the
fruit garden and much
sweeter than sticks
produced later"

# Tree fruit pollination

Some fruit trees need cross-pollination by another variety of the same type that flowers at the same time in order to produce fruit.

Check the pollination needs of a tree before buying it. Look around neighbouring plots to see if they have a tree that will be able to pollinate yours. Pollinating bees will travel as far as two or three miles.

Some varieties are self-fertile, so you need only one tree, although fruit set is still usually better if there is another tree around.

*Pear blossom.*

## Pollination groups

Fruit tree varieties are divided into pollination groups, depending on the time they flower. Choose trees from the same or adjacent groups.

### Apples

Most of the common varieties are in three pollination groups. To complicate things, triploids (marked with a 't') produce sterile pollen, so three compatible trees are needed for all be pollinated.

**Group 2** 'Beauty of Bath', 'Egremont Russet', 'Idared', 'Lord Lambourne', 'McIntosh', 'Reverend W Wilks', 'Ribston Pippin'

**Group 3** 'Arthur Turner', 'Blenheim Orange' (t), 'Bountiful', 'Bramley's Seedling' (t), 'Charles Ross', 'Cox's Orange Pippin'**, 'Discovery', 'Elstar', 'Falstaff', 'Fiesta', 'Fortune', 'Granny Smith', 'Greensleeves', 'James Grieve', 'Jonagold' (t), 'Jonathan', 'Katja' (syn. 'Katy'), 'Kidd's Orange Red'**, 'Lane's Prince Albert', 'Red Devil', 'Redsleeves', 'Scrumptious', 'Spartan', 'Sunset', 'Tydman's Early Worcester', 'Worcester Pearmain' ** not compatible although in the same group

**Group 4** 'Ashmead's Kernel', 'Ellison's Orange', 'Gala', 'Golden Delicious', 'Howgate Wonder', 'Laxton's Superb', 'Lord Derby', 'Pixie', 'Tydeman's Late Orange', 'Winston'

### Cherries

There are six groups for sweet cherries and five for acid; most commonly available sweet ones are in group 4. Some are self fertile (sf), others partly self-fertile (psf) and some totally self infertile (si) so crop only if cross-pollinated.

Sweet cherries 'Bigarreau Napoléon' (si), 'Lapins' (sf), 'Stella' (sf), 'Summer Sun' (sf), 'Sunburst' (sf)

Acid cherries 'Morello' (sf) is in group 5

### Pears

There are three groups for pears.

**Early:** 'Louise Bonne of Jersey', 'Packham's Triumph'

**Mid:** 'Beurré Hardy', 'Concorde', 'Conference' (sf), 'Merton Pride' (t), 'Fertility', 'Williams' Bon Chrétien'

**Late:** 'Beth', 'Catillac' (t), 'Doyenné du Comice', 'Glou Morceau', 'Improved Fertility', 'Onward'

### Plums, damsons & gages

Can be self-fertile (sf), partly self-fertile (psf) or self-infertile (si).

**Group 1** Gage: 'Jefferson' (si)

**Group 2** Gage: 'Denniston's Superb' (sf)

**Group 3** Plum: 'Czar' (sf), 'Laxton's Delight' (psf), 'Opal' (sf), 'Pershore' (sf), 'Victoria' (sf) Gage: 'Golden Transparent' (sf)

**Group 4** Damson: 'Farleigh Damson' (psf), 'Prune Damson' (sf) Gage: 'Cambridge Gage' (psf), 'Oullins Gage' (sf)

**Group 5** Plum: 'Blue Tit' (sf), 'Marjorie's Seedling' (sf)

# Tree fruit

Fruit trees are a permanent feature on the allotment, so it is worth spending time understanding the basics to allow you to enjoy the fruits of your labour for many years.

## Planting

Trees in containers can be planted all year round, although autumn is the best time. Bare-root trees are cheaper, but are planted from late autumn to late winter.

• Before planting, tease out some of the roots of containerised trees and spread out those of bare-root ones. Dig a hole larger than the diameter of the roots and place the roots/rootball into the hole with the top of the rootball or soil mark on the stem level with the ground. Backfill the hole with the soil mixed with compost and a little bone meal. Firm the soil around the roots, water, and then mulch.

• Freestanding trees will need staking.

• Bare-root trees do best with a stake driven into the ground before planting. Container-grown trees need a diagonal stake at about 45 degrees driven in after planting – this avoids damaging the rootball. Use two tree ties to attach the tree to the stake.

## Pruning

Pruning is the key to successful tree-fruit growing: your tree will be healthier and produce more fruit. Different trees need pruning at different times; stone fruit should be pruned only from late spring to late summer, otherwise they are prone to infection from disease.

• Pruning restricts size, but dwarf rooting stocks should always be used to reduce pruning needs.

• Good pruning also creates a stronger structure; unpruned branches can become heavy and snap if overburdened with fruit. Pruning reduces congestion and overcrowding in the centre of the tree, creating a more open canopy. Fruit needs sunlight to ripen effectively, and if there are too many branches they will create shade.

Pruning is an opportunity to remove dead, damaged and diseased wood. Fruit trees are prone to canker, and diseased growth should always be removed.

• The removal of a tree's older branches can reinvigorate it and encourage new, healthy shoots. Don't over-prune though: the tree will produce shoots at the expense of fruit.

• Formative pruning can sculpt your fruit trees into beautiful shapes, such as espaliers, cordons and fans.

## Pruning techniques

• Make pruning cuts with secateurs or loppers just above a bud and gently sloping away from it.

• Large branches need to be removed in sections with a saw so that the weight of the branch doesn't tear the bark below it. When making the final cut, first underscore the branch by cutting about a quarter of the way through the branch from the bottom. Then make the final cut from the top all the way through, ensuring that the swollen collar at the base of the branch is kept intact, as this will aid speedy healing.

*Left* When planting, ensure the rootstock union is above the level of the soil. **Above** Plum blossom.

# MARCH

1. Start sowing tender vegetable seeds indoors. 2. Carefully sprinkle seeds into drills in well-prepared soil...
3. ...or place the seed in the palm of your hand and gently tap into place. 4. Plant onion sets this month.

# This month...

This is the month when things start to get really exciting and hectic on the allotment, especially on the veg plot. It's the first month when outdoor – and indoor – seed sowing can get under full steam. But don't overdo it, and keep an eye on the weather conditions.

It is far better to sow most vegetable types little and often, rather than all in one go. That way you'll have a succession of crops coming to maturity over several weeks, rather than a glut that you can't cope with and then nothing ready for a couple of weeks or more until the next sowing matures.

Part of the skill of allotment gardening is knowing how much to sow, how often and when. It's one of those things that only experience brings – hence 'green fingers' – but a good gardening book helps.

Late frosts and cold weather can quickly put an end to young seedlings, so have cloches and fleece ready to protect them if bad weather is forecast. Fleece will give up to 5°C (9°F) degrees of frost protection.

Another skill is knowing when to sow seeds indoors, timing it right for when the plants are at their best and ready to plant outside, and the weather conditions are ready for the plants too. Leave it too long and plants become drawn, root-bound and rarely crop well; plant out prematurely and they may be at the mercy of adverse weather.

Frost can also damage the blossom of early-flowering apricots, peaches and nectarines, so protect them if possible by covering plants with fleece if frost is due. And if there are no pollinating insects around, you'll have to do the pollen transfer yourself with a small, soft paintbrush.

# Top veg jobs

• Try to avoid digging in really wet weather. If gardening on wet soil, work from a plank of wood to spread your weight and avoid treading on the bed and compacting the soil, otherwise you'll damage the soil structure.

• Cultivate and prepare seedbeds ready for sowing. Work over the soil with a hand cultivator and rake to break soil down into fine particles (tilth). Covering the seedbeds with clear polythene or fleece before sowing will warm up the soil and improve germination.

• Many vegetable crops can be sown directly outside now, especially in mild areas with light soil. These include beetroot, broad beans, bulb onions, carrots, kohlrabi, leeks, lettuces, parsnips, peas, radishes, salad leaves, shallots, spinach, summer cabbage and summer cauliflower, Swiss chard and turnips.

• Most of the above vegetables can also be sown in seedtrays, cell trays or pots in a glasshouse or conservatory for planting out later, when they're big enough to transplant into their final growing positions. This is a good way of getting earlier crops, especially if the weather is too cold to sow directly outside.

• Horticultural fleece and polythene can be used to protect early outdoor sowings and seedlings. Some vegetables, beetroot for example, can bolt (go to seed prematurely) if sown outside too early without protection. Others may sulk in the cold weather and struggle to produce a good crop.

## ALLOTMENT REMINDERS

✔ Put pea supports in place. This can either be twiggy branches or pea netting.

✔ Continue to chit potato tubers. In mild areas you may be able to plant out at the end of the month, although it's better to wait until April in colder regions or where heavy frosts are still forecast.

✔ Check you have enough seeds of all your favourite vegetables; running out in the main sowing season can be frustrating – especially if stockists have sold out.

✔ Finish planting Jerusalem artichoke tubers.

✔ Give spring cabbages a high-nitrogen feed.

## VEG OF THE MONTH – BROCCOLI

**Broccoli tips:** There are three main types of broccoli – white and purple sprouting and calabrese. Sprouting types are hardy and overwintered, calabrese is harvested in autumn.

• Sow sprouting broccoli thinly 1cm (½in) deep in rows 15cm (6in) apart in a seedbed. Thin seedlings to 7.5cm (3in) apart. Calabrese is best sown where it is to crop. Sow little and often during spring and summer to provide a crop for around 10 months of the year.

• When plants are 10–15cm (4–6in) high, transplant to their growing positions, 45cm (18in) apart. Thin directly sown calabrese to 30cm (12in).

• Water well in any periods of dry weather and give occasional summer liquid feeds.

**"**There's nothing more satisfying than sowing some seeds in compost and then seeing the first shoots emerge a few days later**"**

# Making the most of water

Water is a vital resource: all plants need it and rely on the allotmenteer to supply it at certain times of year, especially during extended hot, dry periods. But on the allotment water is an even more vital resource – especially on those allotments that don't have access to mains water. Even then, there are often restrictions on how much water you are allowed to use and some sites ban hosepipes.

That's why it is essential for allotmenteers to make provisions for water supply and, more importantly, water conservation.

*Store as much water as possible coming from shed and greenhouse roofs by installing water butts.*

Not all crops need to be watered and some only at certain growth stages – when seeds are germinating and young seedlings are two critical stages.

Vegetables that produce fruit may need watering only when they're in flower and the fruit is swelling; similarly potatoes will need watering when the new tubers are swelling.

Fruit, especially fruit trees, may never need watering thanks to their deep roots, although in extended periods of severe drought even they will appreciate a good soaking. And the emphasis is on good soakings: little and often can do more damage than good as it promotes surface root growth, which is more susceptible to drying out.

Plants grown in containers will always be more prone to drying out than similar plants that are growing in the ground.

## Save

• If you have a shed on your plot then it makes sense to fit a diverter and a water butt to collect and save water.

• Only water crops that need watering – and only when they need it.

• Use water sensibly.

## Conserve

• Light, sandy soils will dry out quickly, so help the soil hang on to as much water as possible by digging in plenty of well-rotted organic matter and even water-retention gels.

• Mulching the soil around crops will help, and even fresh grass clippings will do a good job, especially if laid on top of sheets of newspaper. But keep the clippings away from stems.

• Dig trenches for thirsty plants and fill them with organic matter, shredded newspaper, torn up cardboard – in fact anything you can find that will absorb and hold water.

# Top fruit jobs

• March is still a good time to plant container-grown fruit, but get it done quickly. As spring progresses and the soil starts to dry out, new fruit plants will need more watering in summer than those planted in autumn. The later you leave planting, the longer you will have to wait for your first crop.

• Make sure the soil is well prepared with plenty of organic matter, such as well-rotted manure, compost, composted bark or tree-planting compost. Mix in more organic matter with the soil dug out from the planting hole and add a general fertiliser, such as bone meal.

• This is also a good time to plant new strawberry plants. Restrict flowering and fruiting by removing most, if not all, of this year's flowers as you want plants to establish properly. If plants fruit too heavily in their first year you may get a much reduced crop next year.

• Place cloches or fleece over outdoor strawberry plants for an earlier crop. Make sure to lift the cover during the warmest part of the day, to allow pollinating insects to enter. A high-potassium feed (such as tomato or rose fertiliser) will help encourage flowers and fruit.

*Blueberries need an acidic soil, but can be grown in containers with ericaceous compost.*

• Pollinate the flowers of strawberry plants growing under glass by using a soft paintbrush or brushing over the plants with your hands.

---

### ALLOTMENT REMINDERS

✔ Finish feeding and mulching around all fruit trees, bushes and canes.

✔ Start feeding container-grown fruit and feed citrus with a summer citrus feed.

✔ Increase the watering of fruit in containers.

---

## FRUIT OF THE MONTH – BLACK CURRANTS

Easy to grow, black currants are packed full of vitamin C. They can be eaten raw, but taste best cooked in pies or jam.

**Currant tips:** Black currants are tolerant plants and bushes will crop in partial shade. The 'Ben' varieties are very hardy.

• Grow black currants as a stool bush: plant about 6cm (2½in) deeper than it was originally growing, so that it sends up lots of shoots each year to fruit the following year and beyond. Plant 1.8m (6ft) apart. Cut back all growth to ground level after planting; if the plant is in leaf, wait until late autumn.

• Prune annually from late autumn to late winter. The aim is to encourage fresh, young shoots, so about one in three of the thicker, older stems are cut back to ground level. Remove old branches and shoots that are lying close to the ground.

**"**Just about every fruit
and vegetable can be
grown in containers,
so make the most of
every bit of space**"**

# Strawberries in 60 days

Although most strawberry plants only really start cropping in their second year, it is possible to have fruit in as little as 60 days from planting. You will have to buy specially frozen plants, which are available from March/April to late July. These will fruit within 60 days, provided they are planted outdoors between May and July. If planted before May they will crop within 90 days.

Although home-grown strawberries taste superior to shop-bought ones, they're so cheap to buy when in season that you may want to try to produce yours when shop prices are at their most expensive.

You can extend the fruiting season by growing a range of varieties that fruit at different times of year. Strawberry varieties can be divided into early, mid and late, depending on when they fruit, and perpetual, which produce at least two flushes of fruit during summer.

*Avoid high shop prices by creating your own strawberry patch on the allotment.*

*Dig a hole large enough to fit the plant roots along each line, then backfill and firm in, ensuring that the crown of each plant is level with the soil surface.*

If you want a crop of strawberries a week earlier than you'd usually pick, place a cloche over an early-fruiting variety as the plants start to flower. For an even earlier crop, pot up plants in the autumn and grow them in a glasshouse over winter and spring.

# Rhubarb pie

**Serves 6–8**

Takes 55–60 minutes

**Ingredients**

**Pastry**

250g (9oz) plain flour

125g (4½oz) chilled unsalted butter, diced

25g (1oz) caster sugar

1 egg yolk

1 egg white, lightly beaten, to glaze

caster sugar, for dredging

**Filling**

750g (1lb 10oz) rhubarb, trimmed and sliced

25g (1oz) unsalted butter

50g (1¾oz) light muscovado sugar

**1** Preheat the oven to 200°C/400°F/gas mark 6. Put the flour in a bowl. Add the butter and rub in with your fingertips until the mixture resembles fine breadcrumbs. Stir in the sugar, then add the egg yolk and enough cold water, 3–4 tablespoons, to mix to a firm dough.

**2** Turn the dough out on a lightly floured surface and knead briefly. Roll out to a round about 35cm (14in) across. Lift the round on to a 23cm (9in) pie plate.

**3** Fill the centre of the pie with the rhubarb, dot with the butter and sprinkle with muscovado sugar. Fold the overlapping pastry over the filling; some of the filling will still show.

**4** Brush the top of the pastry with egg white and dredge with caster sugar. Bake for 35–40 minutes until the pastry is golden brown. Serve warm.

*Forcing a crown of rhubarb in the dark produces the tastiest, most succulent sticks.*

# Root crops

Root vegetables store food reserves in their roots or tubers, and it is these food storage organs that we eat.

## Soil preparation

All root crops like a deep, well-dug, moisture-retentive soil that has had some well-rotted organic matter added. This can be anything from home-made compost, manure or leafmould to spent mushroom compost. The emphasis is on well-rotted, since manure and other strong soil improvers can cause the roots to fork if added fresh. Whatever you add, it is best applied in the autumn or, better still, for a previous crop, to give it time to rot down. The one exception is potatoes, which don't mind too much if the organic matter is added at the same time as planting.

Two weeks before sowing or planting, you can rake in a general granular fertiliser at the rate of 50g per sq m (2oz per sq yd).

Generally, root crops do less well in light soils. These can dry out too quickly in summer, leading to poor cropping, bolting (going to seed prematurely), woody growth, poor flavour or cracking. Stony soils can cause the roots to fork, so try to remove as many stones as possible. On very heavy soils, stick to stump- or round-rooted varieties as the roots don't go down so far.

## Growing

To get the best results, you will probably have to water root crops regularly during extended dry periods. Irregular watering – when the soil goes from bone dry to soaking wet – can lead to cracked roots and reduced flavour and succulence. The organic matter in the soil should help even out fluctuations.

## Raising from seed

Seed-raised root crops don't like to be transplanted or disturbed once growing, so sow seed thinly to do away with thinning out. Or sow a couple of seeds at 'stations' – at the

*Thinly sprinkle root crop seeds in rows (drills) made in well-prepared soil.*

recommended final spacing – and then carefully remove the weakest seedlings to leave just one.

Thin out seedlings at the earliest opportunity: if they are too cramped for too long it can prevent them producing good-sized roots.

Early sowing when soil and weather conditions are not at their best not only leads to poorly developed crops, it can also cause the young plants to bolt, so delay sowing until conditions improve. Alternatively, you can warm the soil for a couple of weeks before sowing by covering it with clear polythene sheets or cloches and grow on your seedlings under cloches or under fleece. You can also sow seeds indoors in cell trays or modules. Starting seeds indoors can give better results than direct sowing of seeds outdoors, especially on exposed sites.

Grown well, potatoes will produce a bumper crop that can be stored for future use.

# Quick-start veg plot

Sometimes, it is better to buy young vegetable plants rather than taking the time, trouble and effort of raising your own from seed.

Having said that, in spring you do need the right conditions for the plants to grow on in before planting out onto the allotment. This means good light and a temperature of around 10–12°C (50–54°F), so you'll either need a glasshouse, conservatory or a good-sized windowsill that gets plenty of indirect sunlight – but not scorching direct sunlight.

Most seed companies provide plants by mail order, but you can also 'top up' anything you've forgotten by buying young plants and seedlings from garden centres and nurseries.

Also, garden centres often have larger plants available in summer – useful if you've had a problem and your plants have died.

Early in the year, young plants will be too small or vulnerable to go straight into their final cropping positions, so they're best potted up first using a good potting compost. Having been grown in protected environments, the plants will need careful nurturing before they can be planted outside. They will need to be acclimatised to the outdoor conditions, or hardened off, for 10–14 days first.

## At home
• When you receive your delivery or get the plants home, remove them from any surrounding packaging (mail-order plants usually come in 'blister packs' or mini greenhouses), give them a good watering and position them somewhere warm and also in good light to help them recover from their strenuous journey.

• Some people make the mistake of trying to remove plug plants from their mesh pots before planting up. This is not necessary and can in fact damage the roots, causing the plants to suffer.

• After planting up, water the compost well and then water regularly to keep the compost evenly moist.

• When handling seedlings and young plants, always hold them by a leaf or the rootball and never the stem, as this is easily damaged and will cause problems later on.

## What size?
You can buy young plants in various stages of growth:

**Seedlings** In spring these will need to be potted up into cell trays or plug trays. In summer they can be planted out into their permanent growing positions.

**Plugs** These are available in spring in various sizes. They all need potting up into small, usually 7.5–10cm (3–4in), pots first before planting out.

**Young plants** In spring they will need hardening off before planting into their permanent growing positions. In summer, they can go straight into their permanent spots.

*Young leek plants should be planted in 15cm (6in) deep holes made with a dibber.*

*The owner of this plot will be rewarded for his well-tended, weed-free crops.*

# APRIL

1. You'll get great results if you sow seeds in pots of good compost with gentle heat. 2. Sowing sweet corn indoors in cell trays.
3. Sow onion seeds in shallow drills in well-prepared soil. 4. Most outdoor crops can be sown directly in the ground this month.

# This month...

If March was hectic, then April can be truly frantic. This is probably the key month of the year for the allotmenteer. Fortunately, the days are getting longer so there is plenty of daylight to help you get as much done as possible on the plot.

A wide range of crops can be sown outside, and as the seeds germinate and sprout, there will be lots of thinning out to do (unless you've managed to overcome the curse of oversowing) and gentle cultivation of everything that's growing – and hopefully growing well.

There are even more vegetables that can be sown indoors with gentle heat. Seedlings of crops sown indoors will need pricking out into small pots or cell or plug trays and maybe even planting out towards the end of the month if the weather's right. Always harden off plants properly before putting them outside: how would you like it if you were thrown outside in cold weather having sat in front of the fire for days on end?

Early fruit blossom may need protection from late frosts; you can say goodbye to this year's bumper crop if the young developing fruit are damaged. Throwing fleece over the plants is all you need to do – and maybe pegging it down so it doesn't blow away.

Sadly, this month marks the time when pests and diseases and weeds start to make their mark. But a little regular diligence will prevent things getting out of control. Try to spend a few minutes at every allotment visit checking for problems and keep the hoe going; dealing with weed seedlings is so much easier than fully grown weeds.

# Top veg jobs

• Nearly all outdoor vegetables can be sown this month. Sow salad crops little and often for a continuous supply. Sow thinly within the row to reduce the need for thinning out, or sow two or three seeds at the final spacing and remove the weaker seedlings if more than one germinates.

• Sow brassicas in a separate seedbed to produce young plants for planting out to their cropping position in May and June. This includes broccoli, cauliflowers and cabbages. It is too late to sow Brussels sprouts, but you can buy young plants for planting out.

• In mild areas you may be able to sow dwarf French beans and sweet corn outside under cloches or fleece towards the end of the month; in colder areas wait until May or sow indoors now.

• Peppers, tomatoes, cucumbers, aubergines, celery, courgettes, pumpkins and squashes and French and runner beans can all be sown indoors with gentle heat in a propagator. French beans may be better started in the cooler conditions of a cold frame.

• Pot up tomato and other seedlings into small pots when they develop true leaves above the more rounded seed leaves. Carefully lift them

*Carefully thin out salad crops.*

from the compost with a dibber or similar, holding the plants by the leaves rather than the stem as this can be easily damaged. After transplanting, water in well and grow on at a minimum temperature of 12-15°C (54-59°F).

• Plant out early potatoes at the beginning of the month; in most areas maincrop potatoes should wait until the second half of April. Potatoes can be planted in deep drills or in individual planting holes, with 5-7.5cm (2-3in) of soil on top. Or, plant them through slits in black

## VEG OF THE MONTH – ASPARAGUS

Fresh, home-grown asparagus is one of those 'luxuries' every allotmenteer looks forward to. Once established, plants should crop for up to 20 years and need little in the way of regular care.

**Asparagus tips:** For best results buy dormant one-year-old plants or 'crowns' of an all-male F1 variety.

• Dig a trench 30cm (12in) wide and 20cm (8in) deep. Work in well-rotted manure into the bottom of the trench, then add some of the excavated soil to make a 7.5–10cm (3–4in) high ridge down the centre of the trench. Place the crowns on top, spreading out the roots, spacing 30–45cm (12–18in) apart. Cover the crowns with soil, leaving the bud tips just visible.

• Add a thick mulch and general granular fertiliser annually in early spring.

**"**Grow runner beans,
sweet corn and
pumpkins all together
to make the most of
space – they're known
as the three sisters**"**

*Sow pea seeds in a shallow, flat-bottomed trench.*

• If frost threatens, cover the shoots with horticultural fleece for protection.

• Plant asparagus crowns. A good, deep, well-drained soil with plenty of organic matter is best for this long-term crop. Plant on a mound of soil and spread out the roots evenly.

• This is a great month to sow peas. Make a flat-bottomed trench 5cm (2in) deep and sow the seeds, spacing them 7.5cm (3in) apart.

• Broad beans grown in pots under cover earlier in the year can be planted into their cropping position. Tall varieties will need some support; place bamboo canes at the ends of the rows and weave string in between the plants and tie off each end to the canes.

• Keep a close eye on plants, especially young plants, for problems with developing pest problems. Aphids can soon get out of hand and flea beetles will attack a wide range of seedlings, especially brassicas.

• Slugs can be a problem at any time, so ensure slug controls are in place.

• Pick yellowing leaves off brassicas to prevent spread of grey mould and brassica downy mildew.

• Damping off of seedlings can be a problem with sowings in containers. Clean equipment and, where necessary, use of fungicides (Cheshunt Compound) can help to control this problem.

polythene sheeting. They can also be planted in containers or potato bags.

• If you planted out potato tubers last month, they may be ready for earthing up to protect the shoots from frost. Earthing up is the drawing up of soil around the stems of the plants, leaving just 5cm (2in) of shoot uncovered so that the plant has enough foliage to continue growing. Start earthing up as the shoots grow, covering them entirely if frosts threaten, and finishing when the earthed-up ridge is about 25cm (10in) high. Potatoes grown under black polythene do not need earthing up, as the polythene excludes light.

---

### ALLOTMENT REMINDERS

✔ Finish planting shallots, garlic and onion sets.

✔ Prepare runner bean and celery trenches if not done last month.

✔ Keep fleece, polythene covers and cloches to hand to protect early outdoor sowings from cold and frost damage.

✔ Pigeons are serious pests of brassicas and other vegetables, so use crop coverings to keep the birds away from vulnerable crops.

# Onion tarte tatin

**Serves 4–6**

Time 50–55 minutes

**Ingredients**

**Pastry**

175g (6oz) self-raising wholemeal flour

75g (3oz) chilled butter, diced

2 tbsp chopped parsley

2 tsp chopped thyme

2–3 tbsp lemon juice

**Filling**

500g (1lb 2oz) shallots, peeled

25g (1oz) butter

2 tbsp olive oil

2 tsp muscovado sugar

salt and pepper

**1** To make the pastry, put the flour in a bowl. Add the butter and rub in with your fingertips until the mixture resembles fine breadcrumbs. Stir in the parsley, thyme and lemon juice and mix to a firm dough. Knead briefly.

**2** Preheat the oven to 200°C/400°F/gas mark 6.

**3** Now make the topping. Boil the shallots in a pan of water for 10 minutes, then drain well. Heat the butter and oil in an ovenproof frying pan, add the shallots and fry gently, stirring, for about 10 minutes, until they are starting to colour. Sprinkle over the sugar, season to taste and cook gently for a further 5 minutes, until the shallots are well coloured. Remove the pan from the heat.

**4** Roll out the dough on a lightly floured surface to a round, a little larger than the pan. Support the dough over the rolling pin and place it over the shallots, tucking the edges of the pastry down the side of the pan. Bake the tart for 20–25 minutes, until the pastry is crisp.

**5** Leave the tart in the pan for 5 minutes to cool, then place a large plate over the pan and invert the tart onto it. Serve warm or cold.

# April

**"A good crop of onions sown or planted in spring can be stored for many months"**

# Top fruit jobs

• Plant outdoor grapevines once all risk of frost has passed. Grapes need a warm, sunny position and deep, well-drained soil to fruit well.

• Sow melon seeds in small pots of compost, one or two seeds per pot; if two seeds germinate carefully remove the smaller of the two. You will need a heated propagator or a warm place for good germination.

• Continue feeding fruit growing in pots with a liquid feed. Alternate between a balanced fertiliser and a high-potash fertiliser. If you forget to feed or if you want to make life easier, treat them to a once-a-year feed with a controlled-release fertiliser.

• Grapevines growing on sandy, nutrient-poor soils may benefit from feeding with magnesium sulphate (60g per sq m/2oz per sq yd) or a foliar feed of Epsom salts, to prevent magnesium deficiency. Pinch out the lateral shoots on grapevines to leave one lateral per 30cm (1ft) of stem. Keep tying in shoots to their supports regularly as they grow.

• Towards the end of the month, it is safe to prune plum, cherry and other stone fruit, but prune only really necessary. These fruit are

*Feathered and furred pests won't like this smart fruit cage, but the allotment management will.*

vulnerable to silver leaf and bacterial canker diseases if pruned too early in spring. Always cut back to a strong, healthy shoot or growing point.

## ALLOTMENT REMINDERS

✔ Keep planting container-grown fruit. Complete planting by the end of the month; fruit planted in summer will be more susceptible to drought.

✔ If possible, protect both plum and pear flowers from late frosts, but allow insects access for pollination.

## FRUIT OF THE MONTH – PLUMS

Most popular plum varieties are self-fertile, but check damsons and gages for pollination needs. Trees should be grafted onto dwarfing rootstocks such as 'St Julien A' or the slightly more dwarfing 'Pixy' to keep them small.

**Plum tips:** Plums need a position sheltered from winds. If your plot is in a frost pocket, select late-flowering varieties, such as 'Czar' and 'Marjorie's Seedling'.

• Grow as a fan on a sheltered, sunny fence panel or south-facing side of the shed, or as a freestanding pyramid.

• Apply a general fertiliser in early spring. Then apply a thick mulch of well-rotted manure around the base.

• Prune plums in late spring or summer to avoid silver leaf disease and bacterial canker.

# Fruiting vegetables

These vegetables are all cold sensitive: one night of cold temperatures when they are young or getting established can severely set them back or kill them. They can be grown outdoors, but aubergines, peppers and some varieties of cucumbers and tomatoes crop much better when they are grown in a glasshouse, polytunnel or frame.

## Raising from seed

Some fruiting vegetables can be sown directly outside in late spring (courgettes and sweet corn, for example), but most will do better if sown indoors in small pots with heat. This ensures plants get off to a flying start and continue strong into summer – essential for good cropping.

Sowing and planting-out times need to be thought about carefully. You don't want to plant them out too early in case they get a chill, but leaving them to get overgrown in their small pots indoors will affect growth and reduce yields.

Thorough hardening off before planting outside is essential to prevent the plants suffering a check to their growth. Gradually acclimatise them to the cooler outdoor temperatures over 10–14 days.

## Growing outdoors

Outside, these crops need a warm, sunny, protected position. The soil should be fertile and well drained but able to hold plenty of moisture.

Covering the soil with clear polythene before planting will warm it up and keep it warm. Do anything you can to protect the young plants while they're getting established outside, including covering them with cloches, glass jars or even cut-down lemonade bottles.

Nearly all these crops (apart from pumpkins, squashes and marrows) grow well in containers; these can either be growing bags or 23–25cm (9–10in) pots filled with good potting compost. When using bags, take extra care over feeding and watering, as their small volume of compost quickly dries out, leading to poor crops, disease and cultural problems.

## Planting pockets

Crops that produce large fruits (pumpkins, squashes, marrows, cucumbers and courgettes) give better results if grown in planting pockets. These hold lots of moisture and ensure large, regular crops. Two to three weeks before sowing or planting out, dig holes 30cm (12in) square and deep and fill with a mixture of compost or well-rotted manure and soil. Leave a low mound at the top of the planting medium and sprinkle a general fertiliser over the soil.

## Feeding & watering

Regular watering is vital: a check in growth can reduce overall yield and quality and cause the skins to harden and crack, ruining the fruit.

It is essential that plants also have plenty of potash – sunshine in a bottle – which promotes good flower production, flower set and fruiting. When in growth, feed plants every 7–10 days with a high-potash liquid fertiliser.

*Marrows are heavy croppers and most plotholders will need only a couple of plants.*

1. Plum tomatoes are a tasty alternative to standard varieties. 2. Winter squashes look attractive and taste delicious.
3. Aubergines are ready to cut when the skin has developed a good colour. 4. Sweet corn is now a regular allotment crop.

# The usual suspects

Unfortunately, you can't grow your own without having some problems with pests. But if you're vigilant, it's easy to nip any problem in the bud before it gets out of control. Take time to check plants – try to do it on every visit. Look on the undersides of the leaves, growing points, flowers and fruit. If you see one aphid and squash it, you'll prevent it from becoming a colony of thousands. Try to squash or remove any clusters of the yellow eggs of the cabbage white butterfly on the underside of brassica leaves before they hatch and your brassicas will stay pest free.

*Cabbage white butterfly caterpillars will quickly damage all brassica plants.*

## Grow organically

You may not want to use chemical pesticides, but even if you do, growing your plants to organic principles will help them resist pest attacks. Organic gardening means getting the soil into best possible 'heart' by adding plenty of bulky organic matter, such as garden compost or well-rotted manure, then feeding the soil and the plants with organic fertilisers. Feeds and tonics based on seaweed have been shown to give plants a degree of pest resistance.

Then use your 'green fingers' to grow your crops to perfection: make sure you do everything you need to do, when you need to do it.

## Physical barriers

Garden or horticultural fleeces and fine-mesh netting are two of the allotmenteer's best weapons in the war on pests. Putting up a physical barrier around susceptible plants will stop the pests getting at them in the first place and hence mean pest-free crops.

Other physical barriers can be used in certain circumstances. Discs of felt put around the stems of brassicas will stop cabbage root fly females laying their eggs, which then turn into root-eating maggots.

## Number one

The number one pests in Britain are slugs and snails. Although you may see slugs on the surface, far more live in the soil – the keel slug being the most infamous example – and do their damage below ground. This means that surrounding your plants with gritty substances, such as ashes or gravel, that are meant to protect plants is useless. Here, it's far better to use a chemical killer, but there are a couple of products based on naturally occurring minerals – aluminium sulphate or ferric phosphate – that are regarded as organic and safe to wildlife. If you don't mind using them, slug pellets applied correctly are safer than many gardeners think.

## Chemical control

Sometimes, no matter how well you grow your plants and how vigilant you are, crops can be attacked by pests. In this case, you may want to use a chemical pesticide. If so, always follow the instructions on the container carefully, spray on a still day so the spray doesn't drift to neighbouring plots and in the evening, when the spray will be more effective and less likely to harm beneficial insects.

*Everyone wants to produce well-grown, pest-free crops. Check plants regularly to keep them free from problems.*

# Crops that money can't buy

One of the great things about having an allotment is that you're in charge of whatever you grow. This means you can choose crops that money just can't buy – or, at least, ones you never see in the shops or are too expensive to buy regularly.

Soya beans are becoming increasing popular. Until recently, they were not a reliable crop in the UK. However, the variety 'Ustie' has been specifically bred to suit the British climate; 'Black Jet' is also hardier than most types and suitable for growing in the UK. They produce lots of downy, weatherproof pods in autumn. The beans must be boiled before eating to destroy inhibitors for protein ingestion.

Or try edamame, now a popular snack in Japanese and Chinese restaurants. The baby soya pods are boiled in water together with condiments such as salt, and served whole.

If you love the taste of asparagus, then the asparagus pea is well worth trying. It is also very ornamental: small, sprawling plants produce attractive, sweet pea-like, deep red flowers followed by curious winged pods. These have the flavour and consistency of asparagus and should be picked when they're about 2.5cm (1in) long. Don't leave them until they're bigger as they become tough and stringy with age.

## Cropping by-products

Some exotic crops come as a 'by-product' of crops you are growing anyway.

You can sometimes find courgette flowers in supermarkets but they are expensive to buy. You can lightly fry them in batter – add a little grated Parmesan cheese first for extra flavour – or you can stuff them with a little mozzarella or ricotta, or even make them into rice-filled parcels.

You can't grow courgettes without having flowers. The female flowers that form at the end of the fruit are the best ones to use, but the male flowers, which should be picked before they start to wither, would otherwise be wasted and are well worth using.

And you don't have to restrict yourself to courgettes – don't forget the flowers of marrows, squashes and pumpkins.

Pea tendrils are a fantastic vegetable when lightly steamed, and a part of the plant that would normally be composted at the end of the year. They can also be eaten raw in salads, used in stir-fries or lightly cooked in butter.

## Weird & wonderful

Salsify is a root vegetable, commonly called the vegetable oyster as it has a similar taste. The roots look like thin parsnips. Scorzonera is similar to salsify, with what is usually regarded as a superior flavour. The edible roots are black-skinned with white flesh.

And don't forget the wide range of Oriental vegetables (*see* page 140), radicchio and blanched chicory chicons.

*Soya beans are now a more popular crop to grow.*

*Courgette flowers – money can't buy these as they don't last long once picked.*

# MAY

*Even though it's a busy time on the plot, take in the sights and sounds and relax in your shed.*

# This month...

Visiting the plot in May is always a delight. A verdant carpet of growing crops now replaces the dull, brown soil of winter and early spring. The fruit section of the allotment is a picture, with lots of blossom and the air humming with the gentle buzz of activity from pollinating insects. It's like being in an English country garden.

Take time to stand, stare and enjoy the sights and sounds of the allotment – but don't let those weeds grow under your feet.

May is also a good time to have a good, long think. Have you forgotten to sow or plant a particular favourite crop? If so, then make sure to remedy the situation now; it'll probably be too late come summer.

As the month progresses, so the number and severity of frosts decrease, and allotmenteers start getting very twitchy about tender vegetables growing under cover. Can I plant them out? Shall I leave it until later? Are they getting potbound? Regular weather-watching reaches fever pitch this month. In colder regions, it can be a risk: a risk that some like to take, but if these tender plants get more that just a whiff of cold weather it can set them back for months. So be cautious. And have some fleece ready for instant protection.

If you have grass paths around your plot, keep them neat and tidy and ensure that the grass doesn't grow into an impenetrable jungle. Not only will it look more attractive, it'll keep any weeds there under control and stop dirty looks from neighbouring plotholders. If you don't have a mower, ask around as there's usually someone who will be happy to let you use theirs – just remember to offer them something in return.

# Top veg jobs

• Sow French and runner beans, squash, outdoor cucumber and pumpkin seeds directly into prepared soil outside – in colder regions you should wait until the end of the month or even early June. Cover with cloches to give protection from cold weather.

• Runner beans benefit from well-prepared ground with lots of well-rotted manure or other organic matter dug in. They need to be planted alongside suitable supports (usually a frame or wigwam of bamboo canes tied together with string) for the shoots to grow up.

• Sow cauliflowers and purple sprouting broccoli in a seedbed, for transplanting out into their final cropping positions when large enough to handle. These will provide winter harvests.

• Sweet corn can be sown outside now or plants that were grown indoors planted out. Sweet corn is best grown in blocks rather than rows, with plants spaced 45cm (18in) apart.

• Continue to earth up potatoes not grown under black polythene (*see* page 58).

• Leeks can either be sown in rows outside in a seedbed, or indoors in modular trays; for mini-leeks sow five or six seeds per module.

• Transplant leeks to their cropping sites when they reach about 10cm (4in) high. Use a large dibber to make holes (about 7.5cm/3in deep) for each plant. Drop a leek into each hole, and then fill the holes with water; don't fill in with soil. For module-grown mini-leeks, each cluster of young plants is transplanted as one unit.

• It is still possible to sow a wide range of vegetables indoors. This is especially useful in colder regions as it will shorten the growing time needed to reach maturity and harvest. Young plants should be planted out once conditions are suitable, and once they've been hardened off (acclimatised to the colder outdoor conditions) for 10–14 days.

• Brussels sprouts for winter should now be ready for transplanting after early or mid-spring sowing. The gaps between plants can be used for short-term 'catch crops' such as radishes, salad leaves or lettuces.

• After the risk of frosts has passed you can plant tomatoes, courgettes, pumpkins and other tender vegetables that were sown and grown indoors into their outdoor positions.

## VEG OF THE MONTH – SPINACH

Some spinach varieties are ideal for spring sowing, others for autumn, and spinach can be grown to produce a crop all year round.

**Spinach tips:** Sow thinly 2.5cm (1in) deep in rows 30cm (12in) apart. Sow summer varieties from early spring to summer. Sow winter varieties in late summer and early autumn. Summer varieties may do better in a lightly shaded position.

• Thin seedlings to 7.5cm (3in) apart, thinned seedlings can be used in salads, or grow as a cut-and-come-again crop without thinning out.

• Grow in a fertile, moisture-retentive soil and keep plants well watered or they will quickly run to seed.

**"**Podding broad beans
is a delight only
bettered by eating
them fresh from the
allotment within
hours of picking**"**

# Growing tomatoes in pots

Tomatoes are a perfect crop for growing in containers. If you grow indoor crops under cover, this is the best way of growing them, otherwise you have to replace the soil annually to prevent the build-up of diseases.

The best containers are 23–25cm (9–10in) pots, but growing bags are still the most popular method of growing tomatoes. But plants in growing bags need a lot more attention: unless you choose a 'jumbo' or 'giant' growing bag, the volume of compost they contain is so small that they soon dry out and the plants suffer as a result. Whichever method you use, regular watering is essential to keep the compost evenly moist; for growing bags this could be two or three times a day in summer.

To get over the drying out problem, some allotmenteers place ring culture pots or tomato growing rings filled with potting compost on top of the bag to increase the compost volume. These are bottomless pots, filled with compost, in which the plants are placed.

Don't rush to plant out your young tomato plants in their final, cropping container: it is best to wait until the flowers of the first truss are beginning to open.

Always keep the compost evenly moist. Irregular watering causes the fruit to crack and split and, together with a lack of calcium in the compost, also leads to blossom end rot – the bottom of the fruit turns black and becomes sunken.

As well as watering, plants in containers will need regular feeding. Either feed with a liquid tomato fertiliser once a week at the recommended dilution or feed every couple of days at half the recommended dilution. Alternatively, add a controlled-release fertiliser to the compost at planting-up time.

Plants will also need a good support system and regular tying in.

*Pot up young tomato plants into small pots once two true leaves have fully formed.*

## ALLOTMENT REMINDERS

- ✔ Continue making successional sowings of salad crops little and often to ensure there is an even supply throughout the summer.
- ✔ Now's the time to plant out glasshouse tomatoes. See this page.
- ✔ Pinch out the tips of broad beans once they have started to flower. This helps to discourage blackfly.
- ✔ Check crops regularly for pest and disease attacks. They can multiply quickly, and early attention will prevent them from getting out of control.

# Cream of asparagus soup

**Serves 6**

Takes 40 minutes

**Ingredients**

1kg (2lb 4oz) asparagus

2 litres (3½ pints) water

25g (1oz) butter

1 tbsp plain flour

pinch of grated nutmeg

2 egg yolks

300ml (½ pint) double cream

salt and white pepper

1 tbsp snipped chives, to garnish

**1** Trim the ends of the asparagus and cut the spears into 2.5cm (1in) segments. Bring the measured water, lightly salted, to the boil, add the asparagus and cook for 15 minutes or until very tender. Drain, reserving the liquid in a jug.

**2** Melt the butter in a large, heavy-based saucepan, stir in the flour and cook over a moderate heat, stirring constantly, for 1 minute. Gradually add the reserved liquid. Bring to the boil, stirring constantly, and cook until thickened. Add the nutmeg and the salt and pepper to taste and cook, stirring frequently, for 3–5 minutes.

**3** Add the asparagus to the soup and reduce the heat. Simmer gently, stirring occasionally, for 5 minutes.

**4** Beat the egg yolks in a small bowl with the cream and add a little pepper. Pour the mixture into the soup, stir well and cook for 1 minute without boiling.

**5** Serve the soup in warm bowls, garnishing each portion with a sprinkling of snipped chives.

# May

"Asparagus beds must be kept weed free, and weeding is best done by hand as the shallow roots are easily damaged by hoeing"

# Top fruit jobs

• Wall-trained peaches, nectarines, cherries, plums and gages can be pruned this month, providing the weather is warm enough for them to be in growth. Wayward branches growing out from the support should be removed entirely.

• Pinch out the growing tips of branches of wall-trained sweet cherries once they have produced six new leaves.

• Shorten the leaders and sideshoots on over-vigorous wall-trained apples and pears; this will divert energy into fruit production rather than leafy growth.

• Hang pheromone traps in apple trees to help reduce codling moth numbers. This is the month when they start to mate, so trapping them will reduce the numbers of eggs. You will need one trap for every three to five trees.

• Several fruit pests and diseases may make an appearance this month, so check plants regularly and deal with any pests accordingly.

• Gently tap or run your hand over indoor grapevine flowers to help pollinate them.

• Thin out crowded raspberry canes. This ensures sufficient air and light between the

*An alternative to strawing strawberries is a weed-suppressing membrane. It also saves on weeding.*

branches to help reduce disease problems and aid fruit ripening.

---

### ALLOTMENT REMINDERS

✔ Feed black currants, blackberries and hybrid berries with a high-nitrogen fertiliser.

✔ Remove unwanted raspberry suckers.

✔ Remove any coverings used to protect against peach leaf curl.

---

### FRUIT OF THE MONTH – STRAWBERRIES

By choosing varieties carefully it is possible to have delicious, succulent strawberries from mid-spring until late autumn; perpetual varieties produce more than one crop per year.

**Strawberry tips:** Strawberries prefer full sun and fertile, well-drained soil. Plant 45cm (18in) apart in rows with 1m (3ft) between rows.

• They will need watering every day during dry periods; always water at the base of the plant, rather than over the foliage. Feed regularly with a high-potash fertiliser, such as a tomato feed, during the growing and fruiting season.

• As strawberries ripen you will need to tuck straw or other dry material under them to prevent the fruit coming into contact with the ground and rotting.

# Peas & beans

**Peas and beans (legumes) need an open, sunny position that is sheltered from strong winds; they are insect pollinated, and the shelter ensures the insects do their job properly.**

They prefer an alkaline to neutral soil (pH7 and greater), so lime acidic soils in late winter for best results.

Legumes need plenty of soil moisture, otherwise the crops are poor or the pods become tough, dry and tasteless. The best way to help provide plenty of soil moisture is to dig a trench roughly 30cm (12in) deep in autumn and fill it with moisture-holding material, such as garden compost, shredded newspaper and garden or kitchen vegetable waste. Top off the trench with soil a fortnight before sowing or planting out.

Water well during dry periods, especially when plants are in flower and the pods are developing. It even pays to mulch the soil around the plants; you can use grass clippings, but keep them well away from the plant stems.

Legumes should be picked regularly. Not only does this ensure the crops are at their best – picked young they have the finest flavour and texture – but it also allows the plants to continue to flower and so crop over the longest period of time possible.

The cropping period can also be extended by choosing varieties that crop at different times (early and maincrop peas, for example), or by sowing at different times of the year (autumn- and spring-sown broad beans). You can also sow seed indoors with a little gentle heat to start plants off early.

## Sowing

Seeds can be sown directly into the soil at the right time of year, but they can also be sown in pots or cell trays and grown on in a glasshouse, cold frame or conservatory or on a light windowsill. Plant out after hardening off for 10–14 days.

Pea and bean seeds don't like to be sown in a cold, damp soil. Broad beans need a minimum soil temperature of 5°C (41°F) for good germination, peas need 10°C (50°F) and runner and French beans need 12–13°C (54–55°F).

## Feeding needs

Legumes produce their own nitrogen, thanks to a symbiotic relationship with a soil-dwelling *Rhizobium* bacteria. As a result, they do not need feeding with high-nitrogen fertilisers, so use balanced or high-potash ones.

A light dressing of a balanced granular feed at sowing or planting-out time is usually all that's needed. A high-potash liquid feed (such as a tomato fertiliser) can be used during the growing season to improve yields.

Nitrogen is released back into the soil as the plant roots decompose, so rather than digging up the spent plants, cut them off at ground level and add top growth to the compost heap.

For more advice on growing peas, *see* pages 24 and 92.

*Pick French beans regularly when they're young and tender to ensure the plants crop for as long as possible.*

Runner beans can be grown up wigwams of bamboo canes to make an ornamental feature in a small space.

# Shed fest

To many allotmenteers, their shed is as important as the plot itself. Not only is it somewhere to keep tools and essential equipment handy, rather than having to drag it along at every visit, it can become a plot social centre. Sharing cups of tea, gossip and hints and tips with fellow plotholders is what having an allotment is all about – it's not just about growing your own.

A shed is also somewhere to shelter when a sudden downpour makes plot care impossible, and somewhere to contemplate plans and jobs that need doing. And, especially for flat dwellers, it can be their only indoor-outdoor living area.

Some sheds are scenes of domestic bliss. Not only are there tea-making facilities, such as a small propane gas ring, some plotholders can even rustle up a full English cooked breakfast and hide away the likes of home-brewing and wine-making equipment.

If your plot currently doesn't have a shed and you want to put one up, check on any necessary permissions first before going ahead and doing so.

Some allotments provide a central shelter, where everyone can get together to make a site visit a social visit and which provides the chance to catch up with what's going on across the allotment. And, if you're very lucky, an organised allotment may even have its own trading shed, where you can buy seeds, fertilisers, composts and other essential pieces of kit, usually at much reduced prices.

Allotmenteers often express their personalities through their sheds, subject to the usual allotment practice of using whatever materials come to hand, from old road-workers' huts to car panels beaten flat.

Sheds are usually placed to the north edge of a plot, ideally where cropping is tricky, such as under trees. They are often grouped away from plots along the sides of the site, to avoid disputes over shade and to keep the site tidy.

*A secure shed will be useful to store all your tools – easier than bringing them to the site at every visit.*

Allotments are often insecure places, and arson, theft and vandalism are common. Because of this, it may be unwise to keep valuable equipment and materials in your shed.

On some plots, patio furniture, barbecues and other homely objects are used to make a private eating and recreational space, often with sheltering shrubs, trees and trellis.

Guttering leading from the roof to water butts gives convenient access to your own water even when the dip tanks are turned off for winter.

Sheds tend to proliferate over the years. Small 'service areas' develop, and things that 'might be useful one day' accumulate. Avoiding this tendency will make your site management committee happier and ease the day when you have to pass the plot on.

1. *Personalise your shed to make it more attractive.*
3. *Set at the edge of the plot, sheds cast no shade.*

2. *Sheds are handy for sheltering from showers.*
4. *A metal hut will not rot and can be used for years.*

# Salad leaves

Bags of cut salad leaves are one of the biggest sellers in the veg section of supermarkets. But why waste money on buying bags of limp, tasteless salads when you can grow your own?

Salad leaves are easy to grow and there are lots of different types to choose from, so go for ones that appeal to your taste buds. Most seed companies sell salad leaf seed mixtures, but you can easily mix your own. With careful selection of types, you can have salad leaves all year round, but for late autumn to early spring leaves you will need a glasshouse, polytunnel or cold frame to provide protection.

## Growing

Salad leaves are fast growing and can be ready in as little as two to three weeks from sowing, so sow successionally – little and often – every couple of weeks to ensure a continual supply.

Because you are harvesting when the plants are young and immature, you don't have to worry too much about sowing density: simply sprinkle the seeds into a shallow drill (row) in the soil. If making your own salad mixes, don't worry about the sowing distance recommended on the seed packet and, of course, there's no need to thin out seedlings, just don't sow too thickly.

The leaves are treated as cut-and-come-again crops by picking a few leaves regularly when needed and allowing new ones to grow back, or cutting down plants close to ground level with scissors and allowing them to reshoot for a second, third or even fourth crop. After cutting, feed with a liquid fertiliser to ensure plants regrow quickly.

## Container salads

All salad leaves can be grown in containers; a 30cm (12in) pot, growing bag or windowbox can provide a vast supply of leaves. Because the plants are only in the compost for a short time, once one crop is harvested, you can sow another crop without worrying about replacing the compost; just aerate it with your fingers and possibly add a little general fertiliser.

## Micro leaves

The latest trend to hit salads is 'micro' leaves. These are harvested when the seedlings have produced their first true leaves. They bring variety to the salad bowl, have intense flavours and can be grown under cover all year round.

Growing them is simplicity itself: the seeds are germinated on moist blotting paper or kitchen towel placed in a seedtray and the seedlings cut with scissors once they're ready.

Lots of vegetables and herbs make excellent micro leaves: try beetroot, broccoli, chard, peas, radishes and rocket, basil, coriander and fennel.

*Carefully harvest the leaves with scissors or snips, leaving the plants to reshoot and produce further crops.*

Grow a range of salad leaf types for a mosaic of colours, leaf textures and flavours.

# JUNE

1. Thoroughly water young plants after planting out.
3. A thin scattering of pellets will deter slugs.

2 Mulch courgettes to help keep the soil moist.
4. The summer is a great time to enjoy your plot.

# This month...

After the manic months of spring, June marks the start of summer and the beginning of a more relaxed time on the plot. Temperatures are on the up, shirtsleeves and even shorts blossom throughout the allotment and suntan lotion starts to feature on the list of gardening essentials.

But, as I'm sure you can imagine, there's no time to sit back and relax on the allotment, especially if it's the start of a good British summer – a hot, sunny summer that is.

At this time of year, it's better to make several short trips to the allotment if your time is limited, rather than spending a whole day there. There will be lots of jobs that are best carried out regularly, such as watering, and pest, disease and weed control. All these things can be problematical if you're there only once a week.

One of the biggest jobs will be watering. Most established fruit crops will not need watering unless there are weeks on end of hot weather, although stone fruit tends to be shallow-rooted and so one of the first crops to show water stress. And if you allow these to dry out the fruit will either abort and drop or it will be small, dry and tasteless.

When watering, make sure you apply enough so it works its way down into the soil where it will benefit the roots, rather than sitting near the surface. Too little, too often will encourage roots to grow near the surface, whereas you want them to grow deep into the soil where they can make full use of deep-seated water reserves.

With vegetables the aim should be to keep the soil evenly moist. Drying and flooding can cause root crops to crack and many others to run to seed (bolt) prematurely.

# Top veg jobs

• Outdoor ridge cucumbers benefit from a site that has been enriched with lots of organic matter to help retain water. Pinch out the tip of the plant when it has made six pairs of leaves, to encourage sideshoot and cucumber formation. Feed the plants regularly with a liquid tomato feed.

• Fruiting crops (aubergine, courgette, cucumber, marrow, pepper, squash and tomato) and legumes (peas and beans) will really benefit from regular watering to help good fruit set and ensure they produce the maximum number of juicy fruit.

• These crops will also benefit from regular weekly feeds with a high-potash liquid fertiliser; tomato fertilisers are suitable for them all.

• As fruiting crops are growing steadily this month, make sure they are tied in regularly to their supports. If left, they can collapse and become damaged under their own weight.

• Remove sideshoots from cordon tomatoes when still small, preferably no larger than 2.5cm (1in) long. The sideshoots develop in the leaf axils (between the stem and leaf), and if allowed to develop will sap the energy of the plant and

*Remove the sideshoots from cordon-grown tomato plants as soon as they're large enough to handle.*

reduce the quality of the yield. Bush and hanging basket varieties don't need sideshooting and should be left to grow naturally.

• Check that the flowers on tomato plants are developing some fruit; if they are not, tap the plants two or three times a day to make sure the pollen fertilises the flowers. Lightly misting the plants with tepid water may also help.

## VEG OF THE MONTH – PEAS

Freshly picked peas always taste the best: that's because as soon as they are picked their sugars start to turn to starch and quickly lose their sweetness and flavour.

**Pea tips:** Round pea varieties are hardier than wrinkled ones, so are best for early sowings in colder weather.

• Sow first earlies in autumn and from early spring to early summer; sow second earlies and maincrops from early spring to summer. To extend cropping, sow an early variety every three to four weeks, or make one or two sowings each of an early, a second early, and a maincrop variety. Or do both!

• Dig out a flat-bottomed trench 5cm (2in) deep and 20–25cm (8–10in) wide. Fork over the bottom of the trench and sow the seeds 7.5cm (3in) apart. Then fill the trench with soil.

**"**The best flavours
come from young
vegetables – so pick
them as soon as
they're ready and
eat straight away**"**

*Chilli peppers need to be tied in at regular intervals to bamboo canes or other supports using soft string.*

• If the flowers of runner beans aren't setting young beans, there are a couple of things you can do to help. Ensure the soil is constantly moist and doesn't dry out; mulching will help. Mist the foliage and flowers in early morning or evening. If your soil is neutral or acidic, water once with hydrated lime. Try sowing a later crop of a pink- or white-flowered variety and pinch out the growing tips of the plants when they are 15–20cm (6–8in) high.

• Water potatoes – especially those that are in tubs and barrels – regularly; if they dry out when the tubers are forming the crop will be significantly reduced.

• Continue to earth-up potatoes (*see* page 58).

• Keep weeds under control. Hoe between rows on warm or windy days to make sure the weeds die without re-rooting. Perennial weeds can be dug up or sprayed with a glyphosate-based weedkiller, but make sure the spray doesn't drift onto crops as these will be damaged or killed too.

• Early-sown crops will start to mature and can be harvested. Don't leave them until the last minute, hoping for the biggest yields. Crops left to grow too large and go past their best tend to lose some of their flavour, even becoming bitter. Root crops may even start to turn woody.

## ALLOTMENT REMINDERS

✔ Continue making successional, little and often sowings of all salad and quick-maturing crops to ensure a regular supply throughout the summer.

✔ If you didn't do it last month, now is the time to sow the following crops directly into prepared beds outside: French and runner beans, maincrop peas, squash, sweet corn and outdoor cucumbers.

✔ Finish planting out tomatoes, courgettes, pumpkins and other tender vegetables that were sown and grown on indoors.

✔ Pinch out the growing points of chilli plants to promote branching and so an even bigger crop.

✔ Keep looking for pest and disease problems and deal with them accordingly.

# Courgette flower risotto

**Serves 4**

Takes 40 minutes

**Ingredients**

900ml (1½ pints) vegetable stock

2 tbsp olive oil

1 onion, finely chopped

1 garlic clove, finely chopped

275g (9¾oz) vialone nano, arborio or carnaroli rice

150ml (¼ pint) dry white wine

2 large courgettes

4 courgette flowers, cut into 2.5cm (1in) strips

grated rind of ½ lemon

1½ tbsp grated Parmesan cheese

pepper

**1** Bring the stock to the boil in a saucepan, then reduce the heat to a gentle simmer.

**2** Heat 1 tbsp of olive oil in a heavy-based saucepan over a low heat. Add the onion and cook, stirring occasionally, for 10 minutes until softened. Add the garlic and rice and cook, stirring, for 1 minute. Pour in the wine and cook, stirring, until the liquid has been absorbed.

**3** Add two ladles of hot stock, keeping the heat to a gentle simmer. Stir continuously until the stock has been absorbed and the rice parts when a wooden spoon is run through it.

**4** Thinly slice one of the courgettes and stir it into the pan. Add another ladleful of stock and continue stirring and adding stock in stages until the rice is creamy and almost tender to the bite. This will take 16–18 minutes.

**5** Coarsely grate the remaining courgette and stir into the pan with the courgette flowers. Add a final ladleful of stock and cook, stirring, for 1 minute. The rice should now be tender, but still firm.

**6** Remove the pan from the heat and stir in the lemon rind, Parmesan and 1 tbsp of oil. Stir vigorously for 15 seconds, then cover with a tight-fitting lid and leave to stand for 1 minute. Season with pepper and serve immediately.

"Marrows, courgettes
and summer squashes
are very closely
related and are
grown in basically
the same way"

# Top fruit jobs

• Strawberries need pampering if you want to enjoy the juiciest of fruits. Water regularly and feed weekly with a high-potash liquid feed.

• Put straw around the plants to prevent soil splashing on to the fruit and spoiling it. Strawberries grown through black plastic don't need strawing.

• Pinch out tender shoot tips of plums and cherries, plus any sideshoots coming from the main stems, to prevent too much leafy growth and ensure good fruit production.

• Pinch out the growing tip of each branch of wall-trained sweet cherries, once they have grown six new leaves. After fruit picking, the shoots can be cut back again, removing half of this year's new growth, and removing any overcrowded or unhealthy-looking stems.

• For wall-trained acid cherries, prune out entirely any fruited shoots, removing all of this year's new growth. Be careful not to remove any un-fruited new shoots, which will produce fruit next year. Instead, tie in so they are easy to pick.

• Thin apples after the natural 'June drop'. Thinning helps improve the size and quality of the crop, and can prevent biennial bearing.

*Pack straw under strawberry plants as the fruits start to ripen to prevent them rotting on the ground.*

• Thin plums and gages after the natural fruit drop, usually at the start of June. Thin in two stages: in early June to 4cm (1.5in) and then in late June to 7.5cm (3in) between fruit.

## ALLOTMENT REMINDERS

✔ Tie in the new shoots of blackberries, loganberries and other cane fruit.

✔ Net soft fruit bushes as the fruit begins to ripen to prevent bird damage.

✔ Ensure there is good air circulation in the glasshouse to reduce the risk of botrytis.

## FRUIT OF THE MONTH – CHERRIES

Biting into the first cherries of the season is an experience you wish could last all year, but choose the right sort: sour cherries are used for cooking, sweet cherries are for eating.

**Cherry tips:** Dwarfing rootstocks make it possible to grow cherries in small spaces. Buy trees on 'Colt' or 'Gisela 5', which will form a tree only about 2m (6½ft) high. Many cherry varieties are self-fertile, so you need only one tree.

• Cherries like a fertile, well-drained soil and sheltered spot. Sweet cherries ripen best in full sun, but sour cherries will happily grow on a north-facing wall of a shed. Grow them as fans or pyramids.

• Cherries are vigorous growers and need feeding with a balanced fertiliser in spring and a high-potash one in summer.

# Salads

Summer just wouldn't be the same without a constant supply of delicious, crunchy salads. But it's not only in summer that salads come into their own, there are salad crops for autumn and even winter. It is possible to produce salad crops all year long if you choose the right mix of types and varieties and have a glasshouse, polytunnel, cold frame or even cloches to help extend the seasons.

Whenever we think about salads it is our recognised favourites that always come to mind – rocket and lettuce being the obvious, ever-present choices – but there are lots of others. These add different textures and delicate, peppery or even spicy flavours to the salad bowl. Try Chinese cabbage, corn salad, endive, land cress, winter purslane or Oriental vegetables (*see* page 140).

## Growing

Most salad crops are fast growing and quick to mature, so should be sown successionally – little and often. Sow just enough for your needs every 10–14 days, rather than all in one go. This not only ensures the cropping period is as long as possible, but it prevents gluts and gaps.

Because they're quick to mature, many salads make excellent catch crops, grown between slower-growing, larger crops to make use of the otherwise wasted ground. Just make sure the salads receive enough light and there are no major differences in the growing needs.

Many salad crops can be grown as cut-and-come-again crops (*see* page 86).

You will need to provide protection for most winter salads in most regions. Hardier crops will stand outside if protected by fleece or cloches, others need to be sown and grown indoors in a glasshouse or polytunnel. If you grow them in pots you can bring them home and grow them on indoors or close to the house for protection, ready to pick whenever you need them.

## Salad care

Being fast growing, these crops should never receive a check to their growth or they quickly run to seed (bolt). To prevent this, make sure the soil is kept moist and water regularly during sunny, dry periods.

In winter, be sure to reduce watering and water carefully trying to keep the leaves dry, otherwise diseases such as grey mould (botrytis) can become a problem.

Although crops will need a fertile soil, don't overdo the feeding, especially with high-nitrogen fertilisers, as this can result in soft, poorly flavoured growth. Soft growth is also more prone to cold damage. Use balanced feeds, therefore, or high-potash feeds that will toughen up the leaves and make them taste better.

*Sow a little seed thinly and often to ensure a succession of tasty salad crops.*

1. Harvest cut-and-come-again crops with scissors. 2. Cos lettuce produce crisp, crunchy leaves.
3. Carefully thin out seedlings as soon as they are large enough to handle to give plants room to develop.

# Allotment friends

Although pests may take their toll on both fruit and veg crops, there is an army of friends you can call on to help fight the war against them.

There are numerous beneficial insects that prey on insect pests and can help get rid of them or at least reduce their numbers. Your best allies are ladybirds, hoverflies and lacewings, although ants and wasps can both do a bit of a mopping up job too.

To encourage ladybirds, hoverflies and lacewings, try to plant a selection of pollen- and nectar-bearing flowers among your crops. Old-fashioned, open-pollinated varieties are usually much better than modern F1 varieties. Flowers with daisy-like flowers are also very popular with natural predators.

Birds can sometimes be a nuisance – especially pigeons – but most bird species will help rid the soil and crops of pests, including slugs.

## Friendly hotels

Unfortunately, our allies sometimes struggle in the depths of winter and will often hibernate in the shed or on dry hollow stems and similar material on the compost heap or elsewhere.

To help them get through winter you can make lacewing shelters or hotels, by making a wooden frame with planks of wood 10cm (4in) wide and 1cm (½in) thick. Once you've made the frame, approximately 10–15cm (4–6in) square, cut hollow stems to 10cm (4in) long and fill the frame with them. The best stems have a hollow diameter of 3–5mm (⅛–¼in). Hang the hotels somewhere that is protected and out of full sun.

## Biological warfare

You can supplement naturally occurring controls by adding your own and waging biological warfare against pests. But don't worry, these biological controls are completely harmless to you, your family, other wildlife – in fact, everything except the specific pest they target.

*Ladybirds are the gardener's friend as they deal with large numbers of aphids.*

Biological controls are naturally occurring organisms that are usually only present in small numbers – too small to have any impact on the pests. But if you introduce reasonably large numbers of the controls, they will seek out and destroy the pests.

Many of the controls need very specific conditions and are only really suitable for use in warm structures, such as glasshouses. Others are very mobile and if you introduce them on your plot, it's likely they'll spend more of their time helping out on your neighbours' plots.

But there is one group of biological control that is very useful outside on the allotment – nematodes. These are microscopic creatures that are watered onto the soil or crop and kill a specific pest. There are nematodes for slugs, vine weevil, carrot root fly, cabbage root fly, leatherjackets, onion fly, ants, caterpillars, sawflies, thrips and codling moths.

Not only are these controls organic, but they do the work for you – just release them and let them get on with it!

1. Hoverflies should be encouraged by planting lots of insect-friendly plants.
2. Lacewings are another ally in the fight against aphids.

# Superfoods

Growing your own is one of the best ways to keep healthy and protect yourself from diseases and other ailments.

It's well known that fruit and vegetables are good for us because they are packed full of vitamins and minerals, hence the government's five-a-day campaign. Both are an essential part of a healthy diet and can help boost the body's immune system, enabling it to fight off some diseases and ailments.

Fresh vegetables and fruits are a rich source of minerals, especially selenium, copper, manganese and iron. Selenium is an important mineral lacking in shop-bought foods, but allotmenteers who grow their own will be eating selenium-rich food, providing they feed their soil with natural fertilisers. Vegetables offer more health benefits than fruit – up to twice as much in some cases.

And although all fruits and vegetables are important, there are some 'superfoods' that boast an incredible number of these essential nutritional ingredients and should always be included on the plot and in the diet.

## Antioxidants
Antioxidants are a group of naturally occurring compounds that have numerous health benefits, including protecting against the effects of cancer and even actively slowing the growth of, and in some cases actually killing, cancer cells. Antioxidants can also fight the effects of ageing and reduce the effects of problems such as cardiovascular disease and Alzheimer's disease.

## Superfoods
Here are the top 10 superfoods:
Beetroot • Brassicas, especially broccoli • Garlic • Potatoes • Pumpkins • Spinach • Tomatoes
There aren't so many fruits that we can grow on the allotment, but **apples**, **blueberries** and the much talked about **goji berry** are all superfruits.

## Making the most of five-a-day – a rainbow of health
Although the 'five-a-day' message has caught on as an important health factor, most people don't realise that this needs to be a good mixture of different fruits and vegetables and that a total of 400g (14oz) of these should be eaten daily. Variety is the key to life as it is important to ensure your five-a-day includes a variety of different fruit and vegetables in as wide a range of colours as possible. The colour pigments in food are made from different compounds and if you eat a rainbow of foods you'll be doing more for your health than you would by just sticking to one type or colour.

Freshness is a major factor in the effectiveness of fruit and vegetables to fight disease, and the best way of getting the freshest produce available is to grow and harvest your own.

*Fruit, such as blackberries, is rich in vitamins and minerals and is an essential part of a healthy diet.*

1. Beetroot is a top 10 superfood...
2. ...as is garlic...
3. ...and as are tomatoes.
4. Blueberries are one of the superfruits.

# JULY

1. Chilli peppers will need regular care this month.
2. Picking gooseberries can be a thorny experience.
3. Shelling the first broad beans is enjoyed by all.
4. Pick beans regularly to keep them cropping.

# This month...

It's the middle of summer, and everything should be growing well on the plot – although how well does depend on how much time, attention and TLC you can give to your plot and its crops.

Make sure all that hard work doesn't go to waste. Don't take your foot off the gas just yet, remain vigilant and keep on top of jobs such as sowing fast-maturing crops, especially salads; watering and feeding (especially plants in containers); plus pest, disease and weed control.

As it's the school summer holidays, this is a perfect time to enrol the help of the whole family. Children can really benefit from days on the plot: they may even be able to use it for school projects, learning about how plants grow, where vegetables come from and the host of wildlife they'll come across, for example.

Having put in the hard graft in spring, you will spend July reaping the rewards from the fruits and veg of your labours, harvesting all that delicious produce that make being an allotmenteer the pure joy it is. Always pick your crops regularly as soon as they mature: don't leave them to get as big as possible, unless you're looking to win prizes in the local show. The best flavours come from the youngest crops; leave them too long and they lose their taste and become tough, stringy or rubbery.

It also means you'll be busy in the kitchen, preparing and cooking some of the best food you've ever tasted.

And now's the time to be thinking about winter, planning ahead and growing all those diehard crops that will get you through the cold, winter months without having to make trips to the supermarket for your fresh fruit and veg.

# Top veg jobs

• There is plenty to harvest, including spinach, beets, carrots, salads and potatoes; shallots and spring-planted garlic may also be ready. Overwintered onions should be ready and can be lifted and used. Pick courgettes regularly before they become marrows. Pick peas and beans as soon as they mature, to stop them becoming tough and stringy and ensure further cropping.

• In hot weather, leafy salad crops may do better when sown in partially shady sites. Hot, dry weather can lead to bitter-tasting leaves. For best results, line the drill with compost, water well and then sow the seeds.

• Lettuce seed is best sown in the cool of the evening rather than during the heat of the day.

• Sow spring cabbage, turnips, Oriental veg, lettuce for autumn, chicory, fennel, and autumn/winter salads such as lamb's lettuce.

• Carrots can still be sown, but beware carrot fly when thinning out seedlings.

• There's still time to sow peas for a late crop.

• Remove sideshoots from upright cordon tomato varieties. And make sure plants are well supported – so tie them in regularly.

---

### ALLOTMENT REMINDERS

✔ Continue making successional, little and often sowings of all salad and quick-maturing crops to ensure a regular supply throughout the summer.

✔ Make sure all vegetables get a regular, constant supply of water to ensure healthy development and to help avoid diseases, disorders and bolting.

✔ Plant out young leek and brassica plants for winter cropping.

✔ Climbing beans may need stopping, to maximise cropping on the existing sideshoots. Stop them when they reach the tops of their supports.

---

• Stop cordon tomatoes once they've reached their maximum height by removing the tip of the main shoot. Look for the leaf that's above the fourth fruit truss and cut it off here. Bush tomatoes should be left to their own devices.

• Non self-blanching celery will need earthing up, after placing a protective collar of paper or cardboard between the stems and the soil.

---

### VEG OF THE MONTH – RUNNER BEANS

Runner beans are an allotment staple: they yield such an enormous crop over such a long time and look wonderful.

**Runner bean tips:** Sow seeds outdoors in late spring and early summer 5cm (2in) deep. For an earlier crop, sow in 7.5–10cm (3–4in) pots in mid-spring indoors with a little heat and plant out in late spring/early summer, after hardening off.

• Make sure the soil is well dug and has plenty of added moisture-holding material, such as compost.

• Plants need sturdy supports to climb up. The traditional way is to grow them up two rows of 2.5m (8ft) bamboo canes, with the bottom 30cm (12in) inserted into the soil. Space canes 20–23cm (8–9in) apart within the row, with the two rows 45cm (18in) apart, forming rows of inverted Vs.

"Digging up the
first new potatoes
of the year feels like
you're unearthing
buried treasure"

# Fresh pea & tomato frittata

**Serves 4**

Takes 20 minutes

**Ingredients**

125g (4½oz) fresh peas

2 tbsp olive oil

bunch of spring onions, sliced

1 garlic clove, crushed

125g (4½oz) cherry tomatoes, halved

6 eggs

2 tbsp chopped mint

handful of pea shoots (optional)

rocket leaves

shavings of Parmesan cheese (optional)

salt and pepper

**1** Cook the peas in a pan of lightly salted boiling water for 3 minutes. Drain and refresh under cold water.

**2** Heat the oil in an ovenproof, non-stick frying pan. Fry the spring onions and garlic for 2 minutes, then add the tomatoes and peas. Preheat the grill.

**3** Beat the eggs with the mint and season with salt and pepper. Swirl the egg mixture into the pan, scatter over the pea shoots, if used, and cook over a medium heat for 3–4 minutes until almost set.

**4** Put the pan under the hot grill and cook the frittata for 2–3 minutes until lightly browned and cooked through. Leave to cool slightly and serve cut into wedges with the rocket and sprinkled with Parmesan shavings, if liked.

# Top fruit jobs

- Branches of plum, greengage and apple trees often collapse and snap under the weight of fruit produced, so make sure you support branches with heavy crops with a stout V-shaped stake.

- Thin apples after the June drop if the fruit is still overcrowded. Remove blemished and king (that is central) fruits from the clusters first.

- Summer prune restricted apples and pears (such as cordons, espaliers, pyramids); in northern regions delay this until August. Prune back sideshoots longer than 25cm (10in) that have formed from existing spurs to one bud past the basal leaf cluster. Shorten new growth directly from the main branch tiers to three or four buds above the basal cluster. Remove spurs or shoots on the central trunk.

- When summer-fruiting raspberries have finished cropping, cut out the old fruiting canes to ground level. As new growth is produced tie it in to the supports. Don't prune autumn-flowering raspberries; this is done in late winter.

- Continue to tie in and train new blackberry shoots. Keep new shoots separate from older, fruiting ones (train the current fruiting shoots

*Apples make attractive features on the allotment when grown as freestanding trees.*

to one side of the support and the new shoots to the other) to make later pruning easier.

- Propagate blackberries and other cane fruits with long, lax stems by tip layering.

---

### ALLOTMENT REMINDERS

✔ Water all fruit thoroughly during extended dry spells, especially stone fruit during fruit set and fruit development.

✔ Cherries and plums can be summer pruned after cropping.

✔ Peg down strawberry runners for new plants.

---

### FRUIT OF THE MONTH – GOOSEBERRIES

Gooseberries are classed as cookers or dessert. In fact, most are dual-purpose and taste sweeter when left to fully ripen.

**Gooseberry tips:** Gooseberries are quite at home in shady areas where nothing else will grow. They need a moist but free-draining soil and will tolerate an exposed site.

- Plant gooseberry bushes 1.5m (5ft) apart. They can also be trained into shapes, such as cordons, fans and stepovers.

- Prune between late autumn and late winter, cutting new growth back to two buds and leaders on bushes back by one-third; pruning new growth to five leaves in summer will also encourage a bigger crop for the following year.

- Keep plants well watered – if put under water stress they are more susceptible to mildew.

**"**Blueberries are easy
to grow and are
full of minerals and
vitamins – grow them
in pots unless your
soil is acidic**"**

# Raspberry meringue cheesecake

**Serves 6–8**

Takes 1½–2 hours, plus chilling

## Ingredients

### Base

175g (6oz) digestive biscuits, finely crushed

50g (1¾oz) butter, melted

½ tsp ground cinnamon

### Filling

250g (9oz) soft cheese

150ml (¼ pint) soured cream

1 tsp grated lemon rind

1 tbsp lemon juice

1 tsp vanilla extract

75g (3oz) caster sugar

1 egg

2 egg yolks

### Fruit topping

375g (13oz) raspberries, fresh or frozen, thawed if frozen

5 tbsp red currant jelly

### Meringue topping

2 egg whites

125g (4½oz) caster sugar

**1** Preheat the oven to 150°C/300°F/gas mark 2.

**2** Mix the biscuits with the butter and cinnamon in a bowl. Press the mixture on to the bottom of a lightly buttered 23cm (9in) flan dish. Transfer the biscuit base to the refrigerator to set.

**3** Meanwhile, make the filling. Beat together the cheese and soured cream, then beat in the lemon rind and juice, vanilla extract and sugar. Beat in the whole egg and egg yolks, and continue beating until the mixture is smooth.

**4** Pour the filling over the base in the flan dish. Bake for 1 hour or until the filling is set. Remove the cheesecake from the oven and leave to cool.

**5** Arrange the raspberries in a single layer over the filling. Melt the jelly in a small saucepan and spoon it over the fruit. Allow the jelly to cool and set, then cover the cake with foil and chill in the refrigerator for at least six hours.

**6** Preheat the oven to 180°C/350°F/gas mark 4.

**7** To make the meringue topping, whisk the egg whites until they are stiff. Whisk in half the sugar and continue whisking until the mixture is stiff and glossy. Then fold in the remaining sugar with a metal spoon.

**8** Spread the meringue carefully over the fruit so that it is completely covered, otherwise the jelly will melt. Level the top of the meringue.

**9** Cook the meringue for 10 minutes or until the meringue is golden brown. Serve immediately.

You simply can't get fresher and tastier raspberries by any other method than growing your own.

# Top herb jobs

There are a number of ways of storing, growing and using herbs. Here are some handy tips.

## Harvest herbs for storing

• To air-dry herbs, tie them in small bunches and hang them up in a warm place.

• To oven-dry herbs, blanch bunches in boiling water for one minute, then place in a cool oven, at 110–120°C/225–250°F/gas mark ¼–½ for 1 hour.

• To microwave-dry herbs, lay out two sheets of kitchen paper in the microwave, arrange a layer of herbs on top, then cover with another sheet of kitchen paper. Set the microwave on high for one minute then check the herbs. Continue in bursts of 30 seconds until they are dried. The whole process should be no longer than three minutes.

• Herbs with soft leaves retain their flavour best if frozen. Pack washed whole sprigs into labelled plastic bags and freeze. You can also freeze herbs in ice-cube trays; chop them coarsely and add one tablespoon of water to each tablespoon of herbs in each compartment of the tray.

## Jobs for the month

• Sow a small pot of basil, coriander, dill and parsley every fortnight for continual supplies.

• Trim bay trees to shape, then lay out the trimmings on a rack to dry for use in the kitchen.

• Take cuttings of rosemary, bay and other perennial herbs.

• Cut back flowered herbs, such as marjoram and thyme, to encourage a new flush of leaves.

## Using herbs

A bouquet garni is a bundle of herbs traditionally used in soups, stocks and stews. The bouquet is cooked with the other ingredients and removed before serving. The herbs are wrapped in cheesecloth or leek leaves and bound with string. Most bouquet garni recipes include parsley, thyme and bay leaf. Optional extras are basil, rosemary, savory and tarragon. Here's our recipe:

1 bay leaf
3 sprigs thyme
4 large sprigs parsley (including stalks)
10cm (4in) celery stalk with leaves
2 x 10cm (4in) green leek leaves

Place the herbs and celery on one leek leaf. Cover with the remaining leaf. Tie securely with string, leaving a length of string so that the bouquet garni can be easily retrieved from the dish.

## HERB OF THE MONTH – THYME

We all have our favourites, but thyme is probably the most useful and versatile herb. Delightfully aromatic and colourful, its flowers attract beneficial insects and the tiny leaves enhance the flavour of many dishes.

**Herb tips:** *Thymus vulgaris* (common thyme) is the most used in the kitchen, but others such as *T. citriodorus* (lemon thyme) provide different flavours.

• Thyme will thrive in relatively poor, preferably alkaline, well-drained soil. It doesn't like wet soil.

• Thyme grows woody quickly, so trim after flowering to keep it compact and promote young growth with the best flavour.

• Snip off small sprigs as needed, or cut larger quantities for drying or freezing before the plant flowers.

# No tears on the plot

The onion family is made up of onions – both bulbing onions and spring onions that are used raw in salads or as a garnish – as well as shallots, garlic and leeks.

The onion family prefers to grow in an open, sunny site. This is essential for those crops that produce bulbs to ensure good ripening towards the end of the growing season. Leeks and spring onions are harvested green, so aren't as fussy and will tolerate some shade.

## Seed or plants?
The onion family is either grown from seed or, in the case of garlic, from bulbing onions and in the case of shallots from young, immature bulbs or sets. Sets have been specially prepared for planting out and are the easiest way of growing onions and shallots.

They are quicker to mature than plants grown from seed (especially important where the growing season is short or weather conditions poor) and are easier to grow. Plants grown from sets can bolt, flowering and running to seed prematurely, but nearly all sets are heat-treated to prevent this from happening.

## Soil preparation
You'll get the best results growing on fertile soil, but if you overdo it and the soil is too rich the plants can produce poor yields, bolt and be more susceptible to diseases. Make sure manure or other organic matter is well rotted, and apply in autumn or winter to give it time to break down.

Applying a balanced general fertiliser at the rate of 50g per sq m (2oz per sq yd) at sowing or planting-out time is usually all the feed that's needed, although an application of sulphate of potash in early to mid-summer helps ripening and improves flavour.

## Growing
The foliage of the onion family doesn't produce a dense canopy. As a result, weeds can easily get

*Allow the tops of the plants to die down before carefully lifting and harvesting the bulbs; these are shallots.*

established and become a problem among the crop. These crops are also shallow rooted, so weed competition will starve them of food and water and greatly reduce yields. So if there's one thing you need to do on a regular basis, it's hoe, hoe and hoe again to keep weeds away. Always hoe carefully to ensure you don't accidentally damage any bulbs, as this can lead to rotting.

Some members of the onion family are prone to bolting. There are a number of reasons for this, but it's usually due to either over-rich soil or a check in their growth. This check can come about from planting out too early in the year, when the weather conditions aren't right, or allowing the plants to dry out during times of critical growth development.

*A good crop of leeks will keep you in green vegetables for several months over the autumn and winter.*

# The heat is on

The popularity of Indian, Thai and Mexican cuisine has raised the profile of chillies and just about everyone seems to have one or two chilli plants growing somewhere on their plots – some grow dozens.

Chilli growing has almost reached cult status, with a degree of bravado attached to eating the hottest chillies. Because of this, there are now seed companies that offer explosively hot ones.

Their heat is measured in Scoville units: a mild pimento scores around 100, while the hottest chilli reaches more than one million. The chemicals that produce the heat are concentrated in the pith around the seeds and in the seeds themselves.

Chillies can be used fresh or can be dried or frozen for future use. They tend to become hotter when they are dried or frozen.

## Sowing

• Sow chillies at 18–21°C (64–70°F) in pots in a propagator or on a warm windowsill. Hot chillies are best sown in late winter, but only if you can provide the heat that is needed for germination and growing on; chilli seed can take a long time to germinate.

*Chillies are ornamental as well as useful in the kitchen.*

• Transplant into 7–9cm (3–3½in) pots when two true leaves have formed and grow on at 18°C (65°F).

## Growing

Chilli plants, especially those of very hot chillies, do better when they are grown under cover as this helps develop the heat and flavour; too much watering dilutes the heat and flavour. In late summer they should be brought inside to ensure good ripening; because of this they are best grown in containers.

Outside, plants need a sunny warm site on fertile, moisture-retentive soil that drains well enough to warm quickly in spring.

• Pre-warm heavier soils either under cloches or under polythene.

• Young plants are ready to plant out once the roots fill the pots. Transfer them to 23–25cm (9–10in) pots of good compost in mid-spring in a heated glasshouse, late spring in an unheated one, and as late as early summer for outdoors. In the ground, space plants 45cm (18in) apart, keeping young plants covered for two weeks.

• Stake plants with canes and tie in as they grow.

• Pinch out growing tips when plants are 20cm (8in) tall to encourage bushiness; sideshoots can be further pinched back to encourage lots of smaller chillies.

• Water regularly and feed with a general fertiliser, switching to a high-potash one when the first fruit has set.

• Mist the foliage regularly, especially indoors, with tepid water to discourage red spider mite and to help flower set.

### Tried and tested RHS varieties
'Apache' (AGM), 'Cayenne', 'Etna' (AGM), 'Fiesta' (AGM), 'Habanero' (AGM), 'Hungarian Hot Wax' (AGM), 'Jalapeno', 'Joe's Long Cayenne', 'Prairie Fire' (AGM), 'Super Chili' (AGM), 'Thai Hot Dragon'

*Chilli peppers are a great crop to grow, as the range of varieties and types is wider than any you can buy.*

# AUGUST

1. Cut courgettes regularly when they are still small. 2. Beetroot looks gorgeous as well as tasting delicious.
3. Marrows are heavy croppers; you will need only a couple of plants to keep you supplied with a good crop.

# This month...

August is usually the best month on the allotment. The weather is wonderful and all you need is a little regular time dispensing TLC to the plot and maturing crops, and you can spend most of the remaining time harvesting bucketfuls of some of the best fruit and veg you've ever tasted.

It's also the most colourful month. Ripening tomatoes in a rainbow of colours, red peppers, aubergines, beautiful beetroot, colourful carrots and rainbow chard, yellow courgettes, not forgetting the red flowers and maybe yellow and purple pods of runner and French beans. In the fruit section, there'll be a riot of colours from burgeoning soft fruit bushes and fruit trees.

However, although you might think this is the time of year to take some time off, you must never transgress one of the allotment rules: 'Thou shan't go on holiday in summer!' Allotmenteers and gardeners can only take a break in winter, when there's hardly anything to do. There really isn't any time to go on holiday – unless you want to come back to an allotment that is parched, with ruined crops to greet you. Instead, make the most of the allotment, enjoy a 'staycation' or 'homiday' and top up your tan on the allotment instead.

With all those crops coming to the peak of perfection, make sure you don't waste any gluts and excesses: it's time to start stocking up the freezer and larder with frozen food, jams, preserves, pickles and dried fruit and herbs. It's also a good time to make friends with fellow plotholders, swopping your excess for some of theirs. Although you may find you've all got too many runner beans and courgettes, so seek out those who are growing fennel, sweet corn or something more exotic.

# Top veg jobs

• Finish harvesting second early potatoes, especially if the weather is damp. In warm, humid weather, blight may be a problem. Cut off the top growth of blighted potatoes and discard to prevent the spread to the tubers; these can still be eaten. Blight also affects tomatoes.

• Harvest sweet corn as it ripens. When the tassels start to shrivel and brown, push a fingernail into the kernel. If the liquid is milky the cob is ready.

• Harvest onions when the necks start to turn brown and papery, and bend over naturally. Don't bend the necks as this can result in disease. Let the tops dry and then remove them.

• Regularly pick fast-maturing vegetables, such as French and runner beans, courgettes, cucumbers and tomatoes, to stop them becoming tough and stringy and to encourage further cropping.

• Summer cauliflowers may need shading to prevent the curds scorching in the sun. Bend the larger, outer leaves over the curd to protect it.

• Marrows and squashes should be raised off the ground (place them on a tile or similar), to stop them rotting from contact with the soil.

• Use fleece or similar coverings to protect late-sown carrot seedlings from carrot fly.

## ALLOTMENT REMINDERS

✔ Keep picking crops regularly as soon as they are ready.

✔ Continue sowing quick-maturing salad crops plus spring cabbage, turnips, Oriental vegetables and overwintering onions.

✔ Keep watering and feeding when and wherever it is needed.

*Home-grown sweet corn tastes sweet and succulent.*

## VEG OF THE MONTH – TOMATOES

There are numerous tomato varieties in all manner of shapes, colours, types and flavours, for eating in salads and cooking.

**Tomato tips**: Unless you have a glasshouse or polytunnel, you'll be restricted to growing outdoor varieties. If you do have protection, you'll benefit from longer and bigger harvests.

• Sow from mid- to late winter to grow in a heated glasshouse, or from late winter to early spring for an unheated glasshouse. For outdoors, sow in early to mid-spring, or eight weeks before the last frosts are expected. Harden plants off for 10–14 days before planting outside.

• Sow at 18°C (64°F) in small pots. Transplant individually into 7–9cm (3–3½in) pots when two true leaves have formed. Grow on the young plants at a minimum of 10°C (50°F).

"Pick courgettes when they're around 10cm (4in) long – leave them too long and you'll end up with monster marrows"

# Raspberry & blackberry cordial

**Makes 2 500ml (18fl oz) bottles**

Takes 2¾–3 hours, plus straining

**Ingredients**

750g (1lb 10oz) blackberries

750g (1lb 10oz) raspberries

150ml (¼ pint) water

about 550g (1lb 4oz) granulated sugar

1 Put the blackberries and raspberries in a large bowl and crush them with a potato masher. Stir in the measured water. Set the bowl over a medium-sized pan, one-quarter filled with boiling water, and cook over a low heat for 1 hour.

2 Mash the fruit again, then spoon the mixture into a jelly bag suspended over a large bowl and strain for at least 4 hours or overnight.

3 Measure the cold juice into a large pan and add 375g (13oz) sugar for every 600ml (1 pint) of liquid. Cook over a low heat, stirring continuously, for about 10 minutes until the sugar has completely dissolved.

4 Carefully skim off any scum. Transfer the cordial to warm, dry bottles, leaving a headspace of 2.5cm (1in). Add tops and seal loosely.

5 Stand a small wire rack in the bottom of a deep saucepan and stand the bottles, spaced slightly apart, on the rack. Wedge folded pieces of paper between the bottles so that they do not fall over or knock together, then fill the pan with cold water to reach the necks of the bottles.

6 Put a sugar thermometer into the pan and slowly heat the water over 1 hour to 77°C/170°F. Maintain the temperature for 20–30 minutes, depending on the size of the bottles.

7 Ladle some of the water out of the pan, then use tongs to lift the bottles out on to a wooden board. Using a cloth, screw the tops on tightly and leave to cool. Label and store in a cool, dark place. The cordial will keep for up to 6 months.

To serve dilute 1 part cordial to 4 parts cold water.

# Mixed summer berry lassi

**Makes about 300ml (½ pint)**

**Ingredients**

50g (1¾oz) mixed strawberries and raspberries

125ml (4fl oz) chilled milk

125ml (4fl oz) chilled natural yogurt

1 tsp rosewater

½ tsp clear honey

strawberry slices, to serve

1 Hull the strawberries. Put all the berries, milk, yogurt and rosewater in a blender and blend until smooth.

2 Pour the mixture into a tall glass, stir in the honey and serve immediately, decorated with slices of strawberry.

# Week Two

# August

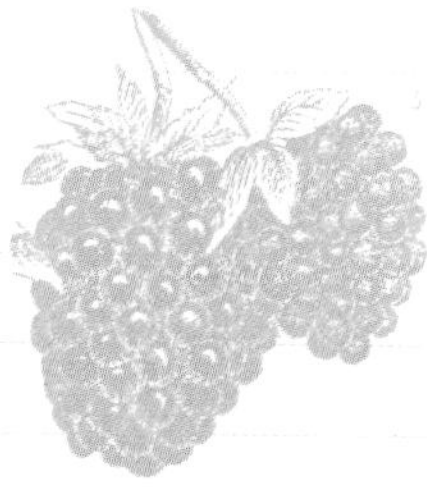

# Top fruit jobs

• Mulching fruit with a 7.5–10cm (3–4in) thick layer of well-rotted organic matter will help retain moisture around the roots as well as keeping weeds away. Make sure to spread the organic matter over the whole root area – an area roughly approximate to the width of the branches. A feed with a high-potash granular fertiliser will help encourage fruiting.

• Prune out any dead and fruited branches after cropping fan-trained plums and cherries, and tie in replacement shoots.

• Any branches growing out away from the wall should be removed entirely.

• If you need replacement shoots for bare areas of an established tree, or if you are forming a new tree, then select and retain one or two strong shoots at the base of the bare area, to train into these areas. Selecting two suitable shoots means you have some insurance in case the first shoot becomes damaged.

• For wall-trained sweet cherries, cut back shoots to remove about half of this year's new growth, removing any overcrowded or unhealthy-looking stems at the same time. For wall-trained 'Morello' and other acid cherries,

*Check fruit regularly for problems.*

prune out entirely any fruited shoots, removing all of this year's new growth. But be careful not to remove any un-fruited new shoots, as these will produce fruit next year.

• Remove fruit affected with brown rot to prevent the disease spreading to otherwise healthy fruit and causing problems next year.

---

### ALLOTMENT REMINDERS

✔ Finish summer pruning of restricted apples and pears (such as cordons, espaliers, pyramids) if this wasn't done last month.

---

### FRUIT OF THE MONTH – PEACHES

Peaches like it hot, making them a challenging fruit to ripen on an allotment. But the effort is well worth it.

**Peach tips:** Peaches need fertile, well-drained soil in a sheltered position. Grow them as fans in a warm, sunny situation, such as on a fence panel or the side of a shed.

• Peaches should be thinned out twice. When they reach the size of hazelnuts, thin to single fruits about 10cm (4in) apart; when they're the size of walnuts thin again to their final spacing of 20cm (8in) apart.

• Peaches fruit on wood produced the previous year. Prune fans in late spring or summer, removing a portion of the old wood and replacing it with new shoots.

• Cut back some shoots to six leaves to encourage new growth.

**"Growing raspberries is easy – not eating them all straight away and having some left for the kitchen is the difficult part"**

# Summer pudding

**Serves 8**

Takes 20–25 minutes, plus chilling

**Ingredients**

500g (1lb 2oz) mixed blackberries and black currants

3 tbsp clear honey

125g (4½oz) raspberries

125g (4½oz) strawberries, hulled and halved

8 slices of wholemeal bread, crusts removed

red currants and sprigs of mint, to decorate

whipped cream, to serve

**1** Put the blackberries and black currants with the honey in a heavy-based saucepan and cook gently, stirring occasionally, for 10–15 minutes until tender. Add the raspberries and strawberries and leave to cool. Strain the fruit, reserving the juice.

**2** Cut three circles of bread the same diameter as a 900ml (1½ pint) pudding basin. Shape the remaining bread so that it fits round the sides of the basin. Soak all of the bread in the reserved fruit juice.

**3** Line the bottom of the basin with one of the circles, then arrange the shaped bread around the sides. Pour in half the fruit and place another circle of bread on top. Cover with the remaining fruit, then top with the remaining bread circle.

**4** Cover the pudding with a saucer small enough to fit inside the basin and put a 500g (1lb 2oz) weight on top. Chill in the refrigerator overnight.

**5** Turn the pudding onto a serving plate and pour over any remaining fruit juice. Decorate with red currants and mint sprigs and serve with whipped cream.

# Stem vegetables

## Celery

If you want to grow easy celery, then choose self-blanching varieties. But, if you have the time, go for 'trench' varieties. You will be rewarded for the extra effort, as these varieties have better flavour.

• To avoid stringy celery, plants must never receive a check to growth, so transplant, harden off and water properly at all times.

### Sowing

Sow from early to mid-spring in seedtrays or pots and germinate at 15°C (59°F).

• Transplant seedlings individually into 7.5cm (3in) pots, modules or cell trays. Plants will be ready to plant outside, after hardening off, when they are 7.5cm (3in) tall or have five or six leaves.

### Growing

For best results, grow above a trench dug the previous autumn and filled with plenty of moisture-holding organic matter. Leave the trench 8–10cm (3–4in) deep for trenching celery; fill it level for self-blanching types.

• Plant 23cm (9in) apart, arranging self-blanching varieties in a block to allow the plants to shade each other to help blanching.

• Water regularly during dry weather and apply a balanced liquid feed every fortnight during the summer. A light dressing of a high-nitrogen fertiliser once the plants are established will help improve crops.

• Mound soil around trench types in late summer, and complete earthing up in early autumn to make a mound with only the foliage tops showing. Alternatively, wrap the plants with corrugated cardboard or similar material and tie it loosely around the stems. In frosty, cold weather cover the tops with straw or fleece.

### Harvesting

Water well before lifting and trimming the whole plant. Lift self-blanching celery from late summer until the first frosts, and the hardier trench varieties from mid-autumn onwards.

**Tried and tested RHS varieties** Trench: 'Granada' (AGM), 'Octavius' (AGM), 'Victoria' (AGM) Self-blanching: 'Celebrity' (AGM), 'Golden Self Blanching', 'Lathom Self Blanching' (AGM)

## Chard & leaf beets

These crops are easy to grow and one sowing will produce an abundant, reliable crop for months. Mainly grown for picking over the summer, leaves can be harvested during autumn and winter and sometimes beyond if the plants are protected.

### Sowing

Sow seeds thinly, 2.5cm (1in) deep and 10cm (4in) apart in rows 38–45cm (15–18in) apart from late spring to mid-summer.

• Thin out the seedlings to 30cm (12in) apart, or 38cm (15in) apart for spinach beet, when large enough to handle.

### Growing

Plants need well-prepared, moisture-retentive soil, but any reasonable soil will usually produce a good crop.

• Water every two weeks during prolonged dry periods. Feed with a high-nitrogen liquid fertiliser fortnightly during the summer if needed.

• In mid-autumn, cover plants for overwintering with cloches or protect the crown with straw or similar material and cover with fleece.

### Harvesting

The approximate time between sowing and harvesting is 12 weeks. Pull off the outer stems when they are large enough to use, and harvest regularly. The thinnings can also be used whole.

**Tried and tested RHS varieties** Chard: 'Bright Lights' (AGM), 'Charlotte' (AGM), 'Lucullus' (AGM), 'Rhubarb Chard' (AGM), 'Rainbow' Spinach beet: 'Perpetual Spinach' (AGM)

1. Celeriac needs similar conditions to celery. 2. Keep the soil moist for a good crop of celery.
3. The colourful and tasty stems of chard are also an attractive sight on the allotment plot.

# Chicken lickin' good

Chickens are wonderful companions for the allotment. Put them on an area that needs weeding and they'll do the job for you, and they will devour slugs and snails and provide a constant supply of chicken manure fertiliser.

## How many chickens?

Three chickens are about the right number where space is at a premium. Two is okay, but never keep a lone chicken, because they are naturally social birds.

• Buy them at 'point of lay', which means they are mature enough to start laying.

• It is not necessary to have a cockerel for egg production as the hens will lay eggs without him.

*Chickens are a great addition to any allotment plot that has the space to put up a chicken house and secure run.*

## Chicken house

A good chicken house must provide a dry, water-tight shelter with a door that can be closed at night to keep out foxes. It must also contain a perch (made from round wood, such as dowelling) for sleeping on and a nest box. Each bird needs a space of at least 15–20cm (6–8in) along the perch.

• Fill the nest box and floor of the house with either straw or wood shavings; avoid hay and sawdust. One nest box is needed for every four chickens.

• Clean the house out twice a month; add the dirty bedding to the compost heap.

## Chicken run

Chickens need a secure outside run where they can scratch around in the earth and give themselves a dust bath.

• The run should be as big as possible, because this is where your chickens will spend the majority of the day. Runs should be made fox-proof by digging chicken wire down 23cm (9in) deep into the soil and turning the buried part outwards at the bottom, away from the run. The door on the chicken run should be closed at night and kept bolted.

## Feeding

Chickens should be fed with good quality layers' pellets or layers' mash each morning. This should be placed in a feeder that can be kept inside the house or in the run. It can be supplemented with corn or wheat as a treat and mixed with oyster shell and grit. This provides chickens with calcium needed to make good strong egg shells, and the grit also helps grind down the food.

They will also enjoy pecking at freshly pulled weeds, fresh grass clippings, allotment pests and any surplus fruit and vegetables and their peelings. At the end of the day, make sure to clear away any food that hasn't been eaten, as this will attract vermin. Chickens must have fresh water each day.

• Consider buying ex-battery hens. They will be good layers and you will be giving a happy home to a bird that will appreciate its new freedom.

• Other good hens to consider include: Leghorn, Rhode Island Red, Speckledy and Sussex Hybrid.

1. Hybrid hens, such as warrens, are good layers, providing an egg each almost every day.
2. Give chickens freedom to wander around parts of the plot and they will make short work of pests.

# A taste of the Orient

Oriental vegetables are becoming more and more popular. There are numerous ways of using them, from adding to salads, stews and soups to stir-fries and as a lightly steamed vegetable. Here are some of the more popular and available ones that add subtle – or not so subtle – flavours to food.

## Chinese mustard greens

There is a wide range of Chinese mustards or mustard greens that can be grown and some are highly ornamental. Less bitter types are used in salads, when young, for their peppery taste while others are pickled.

• Sow seeds thinly from mid-spring to late summer 1cm (½in) deep in rows 25–45cm (10–18in) apart. Some types can be sown all year round in a warm glasshouse or on a windowsill.

• Keep well watered until seedlings appear. When large enough to handle, thin seedlings to 10–30cm (4–12in) apart.

• Sowings made in late summer will carry on cropping into winter if protected.

• Harvest young leaves as needed, picking a few at a time from each plant.

*Used as a cut-and-come-again crop, Oriental vegetables add a range of tastes and flavours to the salad bowl.*

## Mibuna and mizuna

Mibuna produces tight clusters of long, narrow leaves. These have a light mustard flavour, and are excellent in a salad or lightly cooked as a side dish. One of the most versatile cut-and-come-again vegetables, it's very easy to grow and can be cut four or five times a year.

• Mizuna makes a large head of finely dissected, feathery leaves. It has a peppery cabbage flavour. Use the leaves raw in salads or cooked in stir-fries or soups, and the young flowering stems like broccoli.

• Sow at intervals throughout summer outside, or under cover in early autumn. You can sow directly where the plants are to grow, in a seedbed and then transfer plants to their growing positions, or in pots or module trays and then plant out.

• Both crops are harvested in more than one way. Plants to be used when young should be 10–15cm (4–6in) apart, those to be cut frequently for their leaves 20cm (8in) apart and those for larger plants 30–40cm (12–16in) apart.

• Keep plants well watered in dry periods.

## Pak choi

Pak choi is used in salads or stir-fries as a baby leaf. When semi-mature or fully grown, it's cooked in a variety of Oriental dishes.

• Pak choi grows best in a sunny position in a fertile soil. Sow thinly 1cm (½in) deep in rows 30–38cm (12–15in) apart from late spring to mid-summer; the older you want to harvest, the wider the spacing.

• Make earlier and later sowings for baby leaves under protection in mild areas.

• Gradually thin to 7.5–10cm (3–4in) for baby leaf, 20cm (8in) for semi-mature plants and to 25–30cm (10–12in) for mature plants. Keep plants well watered to avoid bolting and blandness.

*Oriental vegetables, such as mustard spinach, are versatile crops that have numerous uses in the kitchen.*

# SEPTEMBER

1. It's easy to grow a good crop of apples. 2. Courgettes are prolific cropping plants.
3. This is the last month tomatoes will ripen naturally. 4. Squashes are available in a range of tasty types.

# This month...

September marks the beginning of autumn, the season of fruitful bounty, but the weather can still be warm and Indian summers are common. So there's plenty of time to spend long, happy days on the allotment. Make the most of the good weather: there are still jobs to do and lots of crops to harvest, and maybe you can make a start on those all-important winter preparations.

Although the bright colours of summer are diminishing, there's impact from ripening tomatoes, peppers and the beginning of those great autumn and winter stalwarts – squashes, marrows and pumpkins. All of these will need to make full use of the sun to ripen perfectly for both eating and storing.

And, of course, the colour from apples and pears comes to the fore and picking and scoffing straight from the tree is an autumn delight. If you're growing autumn raspberries, these little jewels of explosive flavour are a much-anticipated delight.

As things start to slow down and crops finish, this is the time to take pride in your plot and start the big autumn tidy up. If you haven't already – but as a proud allotmenteer, you surely will have – ensure that you have plenty of compost heaps on the go. All that end-of-season vegetation will make fantastic soil-improving and mulching material and is a bounty not to be wasted.

This is also the last major month when weeds can raise their ugly heads above the soil. Clearing them away as soon as they're seen and never letting them flower and set seed will ensure you spend less time controlling this time-consuming allotment problem in the future. Forward planning is the key to success for a thriving allotment plot.

# Top veg jobs

- Sow green manures, such as mustard and Italian ryegrass, to prevent autumn weeds establishing, soil nutrients washing away and to act as a soil improver when dug in during early spring. Or, after clearing away finished crops, cover bare soil with black plastic sheeting to suppress weeds and prevent the soil becoming waterlogged.

- Once summer crops come to an end, the plants should be consigned to the compost heap. The best compost comes from using a wide range of ingredients, well mixed together. Any large material, such as Brussels sprout stems or runner bean plants, should be cut up into small pieces to speed up composting.

- Don't stop feeding tomatoes still in crop: liquid feeds will help ripen the last fruits of the season.

- Remaining outdoor tomatoes should be picked by the end of the month and ripened indoors. The whole truss can be cut off to allow the fruit to ripen 'on the vine' on a windowsill. Green fruit that won't ripen can be made into chutneys.

- Earth up, or add to the cardboard sheath over any remaining trench celery plants that have not yet had their final top-up. Only a tuft of foliage should show at the top.

## ALLOTMENT REMINDERS

✔ Start digging over vacant areas of the vegetable plot, especially those on clay soil, adding well-rotted compost if necessary.

✔ Sow overwintering turnip and onions, spinach, winter lettuce and Oriental veg.

✔ Plant overwintering onion sets.

✔ Finish lifting and drying onions and potatoes.

✔ Continue to water winter squashes and pumpkins in growth to give bumper crops.

## VEG OF THE MONTH – SWEET CORN

Sweet corn is a fast-maturing, tender vegetable, so make sure it isn't hit by cold weather and frosts in spring. Late planting will not affect the yield as it needs a relatively short growing season.

**Sweet corn tips:** Sow seed individually from mid- to late spring at 18–21°C (64–70°F) in deep pots at a depth of 2.5cm (1in). You can sow seed direct outside from late spring to early summer in soil pre-warmed under clear plastic covers. Leave the covers over the plants until the plants have grown and touch the top.

- Plant out indoor-raised plants at the very end of spring or start of summer.

- Sweet corn must be grown in a sunny position, sheltered from strong wind. The plants are wind-pollinated, so grow them in blocks, with plants spaced 38–45cm (15–18in) apart.

# September

**"Don't waste any of your precious harvest – get busy in the kitchen freezing excesses, and making pies, soups, chutneys and preserves"**

# Green tomato chutney

**Makes about 2kg (4lb 8oz)**

Takes 1¾–2 hours

**Ingredients**

1kg (2lb 4oz) green tomatoes, finely chopped

500g (1lb 2oz) onions, finely chopped

500g (1lb 2oz) cooking apples, peeled, cored and chopped

2 fresh green chillies, halved, deseeded and finely chopped

2 garlic cloves, crushed

1 tsp ground ginger

generous pinch of ground cloves

generous pinch of ground turmeric

50g (1¾oz) raisins

250g (9oz) soft dark brown sugar

300ml (½ pint) white wine vinegar

**1** Put the tomatoes, onions, apples and chillies into a large saucepan and mix together. Add the garlic, ginger, cloves and turmeric, then stir in the raisins, sugar and vinegar.

**2** Bring the mixture to the boil, reduce the heat and cover the pan. Simmer, stirring frequently, for 1¼–1½ hours or until the chutney has thickened.

**3** Transfer the chutney to warm, dry jars. Cover the surface of each one with a disc of waxed paper, waxed side down, then top with an airtight lid.

**4** Label and leave to mature in a cool, dark place for at least 3 weeks before using, or store, unopened, for 6–12 months.

# Top fruit jobs

• Regularly pick all fruit as it becomes ready. Don't leave it on the tree or bush to become overripe, but don't pick too early or the full flavour won't have developed. Most fruit is ready when it comes away easily in the hand.

• Apples and pears are generally ready to pick when they readily part from the tree when lifted gently in the palm and given a slight twist. Pears are best picked when slightly immature. They should then be left a couple of days at room temperature to reach full maturity.

• Apple trees may have produced strong vertical shoots (called water shoots) from old branches. Cut out or thin out this unproductive growth entirely as soon as possible.

• Cut out fruited canes of summer raspberries and tie in new canes that will fruit next year. Select strong, healthy canes and cut out any weak, forked or misplaced ones.

• Cut out the old canes of blackberries and hybrid berries after fruiting and tie in new ones formed this year that will fruit next year.

• Water new strawberry beds planted this season. If you have not yet planted new beds, this is the last chance this year to do so.

*Yellow-fruited raspberries are different and delicious.*

• Propagate blackberries and other cane fruits with long, lax stems by tip layering. Weigh down the tip of a shoot into the soil or into a sunken pot full of compost with a stone; only layer shoots from productive plants.

---

## ALLOTMENT REMINDERS

✔ Finish tying in shoots on wall-trained fan trees. It's too late to prune stone fruit.

✔ Lift and pot up or plant out rooted strawberry runners.

✔ If bacterial canker has been a problem, spray with a copper-based fungicide.

---

## FRUIT OF THE MONTH – BLUEBERRIES

Blueberries are a superb addition to the plot. The fruit has lots of health benefits and they are a 'superfood' (see page 104).

**Blueberry tips:** Blueberries need a sheltered, sunny site with moist but well-drained soil. They need an acidic soil, so if your soil has a pH higher than 5.5 you will need to grow them in containers or in a raised or sunken bed. It is possible to change the existing soil using acidifying materials, such as sulphur chips. Plant bushes 1–1.2m (3–4ft) apart.

• Raised/sunken beds should be 60cm (2ft) deep and lined with polythene, pierced in a few places to allow drainage. Fill with neutral or acidic soil mixed with equal parts of ericaceous compost and composted bark. Grow in containers using a loam-based ericaceous potting compost.

**"**Home-grown pears
are best eaten in the
bath — they're so juicy,
it's the easiest way
to stay clean!**"**

# Blackberry & apple jam

**Makes about 3.25kg (7lb)**

Takes 1½ hours, plus standing

**Ingredients**

1kg (2lb 4oz) slightly under-ripe blackberries,
stalks discarded

1.75kg (3lb 12oz) sugar

1kg (2lb 4oz) cooking apples

300ml (½ pint) water

125ml (4fl oz) lemon juice

**1** Rinse the blackberries, allow to dry and layer
in a large bowl with the sugar. Leave the fruit to
stand overnight.

**2** Peel, core and slice the apples. Place all
the trimmings in a pan and pour in the water.
Bring to the boil and boil, uncovered, for
about 20 minutes until most of the water

has evaporated and the trimmings are pulpy.
Press the mixture through a fine sieve into
a large pan.

**3** Add the apple slices to the pan and pour
in the blackberries with all their juice and any
undissolved sugar. Heat the mixture gently to
simmering point, stirring the pan continuously
for about 10 minutes until the sugar has
completely dissolved and all the fruit is soft.
Add the lemon juice.

**4** Bring the jam to the boil and boil hard to
setting point. Remove from the heat and
carefully skim off any scum.

**5** Transfer the jam to warm, dry jars. Cover the
surface of each one with a disc of waxed paper,
waxed side down, then top with an airtight lid or
cellophane cover. Label and leave to cool, then
store in a cool, dark place.

The jam will keep for 3–4 months.

# Brassicas

Brassicas, the cabbage family, are important vegetables. They can provide nutritious crops just about all year round, but particularly from winter to early spring when very little else is available fresh.

Brassicas include cabbage and kale, cauliflower, Brussels sprouts, broccoli and calabrese, plus the root crops kohlrabi, swedes and turnips. All share similar needs and problems, so they should be grown together in crop rotations.

## Growing

Brassicas prefer a sunny site, although cabbages, Brussels sprouts and kale tolerate light shade. They prefer a humus-rich, alkaline soil, of pH6–7.5; if your soil is acidic add lime before sowing or planting out.

Leafy brassicas also need the soil in their final growing positions to be firm and reasonably well compacted to produce solid, firm hearts or heads. Walk over the soil with your weight on your heels before planting out.

In exposed sites it pays to earth up around the stems of overwintering plants – especially those of Brussels sprouts – or tie them to stout canes or stakes.

## Raising from seed

All brassicas need a soil temperature of at least 7°C (45°F) to germinate. With leafy brassicas, you'll get better results if you can set aside a small area as a seedbed, sowing and growing them on here before transplanting the young plants to their final positions.

If you don't have room for a seedbed, want to produce earlier crops, or find that seed-sown plants struggle when sown directly outside, raise the young plants in cell or module trays in a glasshouse, conservatory or cold frame, or on a windowsill. Providing gentle heat will give better results when sowing in winter or early spring. Sow two seeds per module and remove the weakest seedling if both germinate.

Plants grown indoors need to be hardened off or acclimatised for 10–14 days before planting out.

When plants raised outside are big enough, usually when they have developed five or six true leaves, transplant them into their final growing places. Water them well the day before to reduce shock and lift them with as much soil as possible.

Before planting out add a general, balanced, granular fertiliser and rake in. Some brassicas can be very sensitive to a lack of trace elements in the soil, especially boron and manganese, so using a fertiliser that contains these trace elements or micronutrients often gives even better results.

Transplant into a hole deep enough for the young plant's lower leaves to touch the soil. Puddle in by filling the hole with water before filling it with soil and firming around the plant.

*Brussels sprouts may need staking to prevent them blowing over on exposed allotment sites.*

A good cage, covered in mesh netting, will keep rabbits and pigeons away from prized overwintering crops.

# Storing crops

Several allotment staples can be stored in a cool, dry cellar, shed or garage to provide food supplies over the winter months. Store only sound and disease-free crops, otherwise in-store rots can set in, which can ruin the whole lot. Check them regularly: any that are showing signs of rotting should be disposed of immediately before it spreads to sound ones.

## Apples

Early apple varieties won't store and need to be eaten within one or two days of picking. Later varieties can last for months, if kept properly. A slight humidity also helps to preserve the fruit. Ideal temperatures are 2–5°C (36–41°F). Good ventilation is important, so store apples in slatted wooden or plastic crates or boxes, spreading the fruit out evenly and ensuring they do not touch each other. The fruit can also be wrapped in paper to help prevent contact.

## Pears

Pears benefit from storage or a period of ripening before eating: early varieties usually need a week or so until they become softer, while later ones can need months before being ready for eating. Carefully press the pear for softness, particularly around the stalk, for indications of the fruit being ready for eating. Pears tend to rot very quickly so regular inspections of the fruit are imperative. Store pears in the same way you store apples.

## Onions

Onions for storage need to be handled carefully when ready for harvesting to make sure that they store well.

Bending over the foliage or gently lifting the bulbs to break the roots is no longer recommended. Once the foliage has turned yellow, leave the plants for two to three weeks and then carefully lift them with a garden fork on a dry day.

It is best to remove the tops once the plants have been lifted. Cut off the top 5–7.5cm (2–3in) above the neck to speed up drying and reduce the likelihood of rot. Cut off the roots and remove loose or split skins, but don't remove too many layers or it will hinder ripening.

Onions need drying for two to three weeks, either laid out in the sun or over wire mesh in a shed. Once dry, store in trays with slatted bases, net bags or old tights for good air circulation, or tie an onion rope.

## Potatoes

Although it's usually maincrops that are stored, it is possible to store early varieties, although they generally won't last as long as maincrops. Carefully dig up the potatoes with a garden fork to avoid damaging them. Leave to dry on the ground for a few hours before storing and carefully rub off loose soil. Store only sound tubers in paper or hessian sacks or in well-ventilated dark boxes.

## Marrows, pumpkins & winter squashes

Let the fruit mature on the plant for as long as possible, to ensure the best flavour develops, but cut and remove before the first frost strikes.

Place somewhere warm and sunny for seven to 10 days so that the skin 'cures' and hardens, to help prevent rotting in store.

When ready, store in a dark, cool, dry but frost-free place. Place the fruit in single layers on cardboard or, better still, wooden slats to allow good air circulation. If space is limited, you can stack them no more than three fruit high, preferably only two, but check regularly for rotting.

*1. Apples can be stored for several months over autumn and winter. 2. Pears benefit from storage or a period of ripening.
3. Dry onions in the sun for a couple of weeks before storing. 4. Similarly, potatoes need a few hours' drying.*

# OCTOBER

*A productive plot can also be attractive – and both sedum and sage will attract beneficial insects to the allotment.*

# This month...

Although there's a definite nip in the air, October is a great time on the allotment. Everything starts to quieten down and you can do things at your own pace, rather than being dominated by the demands of your crops.

Apples and pears and pumpkins and squashes come into the peak of their harvest, autumn and winter root crops are ready and you can lick your lips at the thought of hearty roasted vegetable dishes for dinner.

Plummeting temperatures usually follow warm days and clear skies this month. If the first severe frost strikes in October it will put a sudden end to all those tender vegetables. So keep an eye on that thermometer and make sure you harvest anything that could be finished off by a cold spell. And if you do get caught out, a quick covering with fleece will give you a few days' grace to get the job done without wasting further harvests. The last of the tomatoes, peppers and aubergines will go to make a fabulous, tasty ratatouille, so make lots and freeze any you can't eat straight away.

And if you run out of hot tea in your vacuum flask and need to do some gentle exercise on the plot to keep warm, then there's always a spot of digging to do. Heavy, clay soils become compacted over the summer and the airless soil can result in poor crops the following year. Digging over not only gets some essential air back into the soil, but it also gives you the chance to remove perennial weeds, the birds the chance to remove soil pests and the frosts and cold weather the chance to break them down and produce a better, vegetable-friendly structure.

# Top veg jobs

• Most autumn and winter root vegetables are best left in the ground and gathered as needed, but to guard against cold spells preventing harvesting or causing damage, lift some and store in a cool, frost-free shed. Celeriac and turnips are especially frost sensitive. Carrots left in the ground benefit from an insulating covering of straw or similar under plastic sheeting. Parsnips produce sweeter roots if they are exposed to frosts.

• In cold districts, carrots, beetroot and turnip are best lifted and stored for winter.

• Harvest pumpkins and winter squashes when ripe (*see* page 156).

• Dig up outdoor tomato plants and hang them upside-down in the greenhouse to allow the fruits to ripen. Any that don't ripen can be brought inside and ripened in a drawer with a banana or used to make green tomato chutney.

• Carrots and peas can still be sown in cold frames, but only in mild areas.

• Radishes, mustard cress and winter lettuces can be sown in growing bags in a glasshouse.

• Cut the dying tops of Jerusalem artichokes to ground level, and harvest tubers as needed.

*Parsnips are one of the joys of the autumn harvest.*

## ALLOTMENT REMINDERS

✔ Finish planting autumn onion sets.

✔ Finish earthing up trench celery.

✔ Earth up or stake Brussels sprout plants to stop them being blown over in strong winds.

✔ In mild areas, sow green manures including field beans, winter tares and Italian ryegrass.

✔ Finish planting out spring cabbages to their final positions. Cover with horticultural fleece or netting to stop the pigeons getting to them.

## VEG OF THE MONTH – PUMPKINS

These are big, beefy spreading plants that need a lot of room, which is great if you have soil to cover up.

**Pumpkin tips:** Sow seeds from mid- to late spring on their sides 1cm (½in) deep individually in 7.5cm (3in) pots of compost. Keep in a propagator or warm place at 18–21°C (64–70°F).

• Outside, sow seeds 2.5cm (1in) deep in late spring or early summer and cover with cloches or jars. Leave these in place for two weeks after germination.

• Pumpkins and winter squashes need a sunny, sheltered position and a fertile, moisture-retentive soil.

• For best results, grow them in planting pockets (*see* page 64).

• Water around the plants, not over them. Feed every 10–14 days with a high-potash liquid fertiliser once the fruit starts to swell.

**"**The giants of the
veg patch – pumpkins
and squashes – are
versatile, delicious
autumn kitchen
staples and deserve
to be widely grown**"**

# Baked autumn roots with mixed spices

**Serves 6**

Takes 50–55 minutes

**Ingredients**

1 tsp fennel seeds

1 tsp cumin seeds

1 tsp coriander seeds

½ tsp turmeric

½ tsp paprika

2 garlic cloves, chopped

3 tbsp olive oil

salt and pepper

500g (1lb 2oz) butternut squash, peeled, halved, deseeded and thickly sliced

4 small parsnips, about 425g (15oz) in total, cut into quarters

3 carrots, about 300g (10½oz) in total, cut into thick strips

**1** Preheat the oven to 200°C/400°F/gas mark 6.

**2** Crush the seeds using a pestle and mortar or the end of a rolling pin. Turn them into a large plastic bag and add the turmeric, paprika, garlic, oil and salt and pepper. Fasten the bag and shake to mix the spices together.

**3** Add the vegetables to the plastic bag, grip the top edge to seal and toss together until the vegetables are coated with the spices.

**4** Tip the vegetables into a roasting tin and bake for 35–40 minutes, turning once, until browned and tender. Transfer to a serving dish.

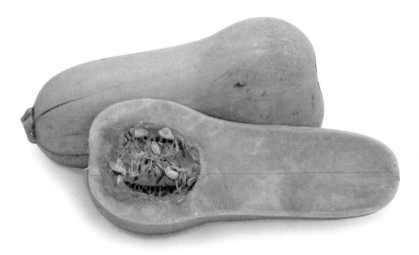

# Top fruit jobs

- Harvest apples and pears for eating or storing. Store only unblemished fruit to prevent it rotting in storage.

- Take hardwood cuttings of blueberries, currants, gooseberries, figs and grapevines; use only healthy, virus-free plants.

- Remove strong, healthy-looking shoots about 23–30cm (9–12in) long. Trim the base just below a bud and trim the top to just above a bud, removing the soft growing tip. Treat the bottom cut with hormone rooting powder or liquid. Insert the cuttings to half to two-thirds their height in a V-shaped hole, lined with 2.5cm (1in) sharp sand or grit. Make the hole by inserting a spade into the ground and then pushing it forward. The cuttings will have rooted and be ready to plant out next autumn.

- In cold regions, you may need to provide winter protection for wall-trained figs to help the young figs overwinter to produce next year's crop. Cover them with plastic netting and fill between the plant and the netting with straw, bracken or other open material. This covering should remain on until the danger of frost has passed in spring.

- Do not let fallen apple, pear, plum and peach leaves infected with diseases lie on the ground – rake them up as soon as possible. Good hygiene is critical in the control of common problems.

- Prevent damage to apples next year by applying grease bands to the trunks of trees to stop adults of the wingless moth climbing up to lay eggs. Tree stakes will also need grease-banding if they provide a route for the moths into the branches.

- Spray peach and nectarine plants as the leaves fall with a copper-based fungicide to protect against peach leaf curl.

- Clean up old strawberry beds, removing yellow foliage, straw, old runners and any plants that look as if they may have virus.

---

**ALLOTMENT REMINDERS**

✔ Continue to remove and destroy apples, pears and plums affected with brown rot to prevent the disease from spreading.

---

## FRUIT OF THE MONTH – PEARS

Succulent fruit with soft, melting flesh make pears a popular fruit. Grow as cordons, espaliers, pyramids and bushes.

**Pear tips:** Pears usually need a partner to help with pollination; look at the pollination groups on page 30.

- Pears need a sunny site that is sheltered from prevailing winds. Grow later-flowering varieties such as 'Beth' or 'Doyenné du Comice' if frost is a problem.
- Pears need plenty of moisture during summer.
- Trees trained as cordons and espaliers need new growth pruned back to two buds in late summer. Thin out the spurs in winter. Prune bush trees in winter, removing low-growing, diseased or dead wood and branches growing into the centre.
- Pears should be picked when slightly under-ripe.

**"**Get your own plants
for free – propagate
new fruit bushes from
hardwood cuttings**"**

# Pear & cardamom flan

**Serves 6**

Takes 1½–1¾ hours, plus chilling

**Ingredients**

**Pastry**

175g (6oz) plain flour

¼ tsp salt

100g (3½oz) unsalted butter, diced, plus extra for greasing

2 tbsp caster sugar

1 egg yolk

**Filling**

125g (4½oz) unsalted butter, softened

75g (3oz) caster sugar

2 small eggs, lightly beaten

75g (3oz) ground hazelnuts

25g (1oz) ground rice

seeds from 2 cardamom pods, crushed

1 tsp grated lemon rind

4 tbsp soured cream

3 small firm pears

**1** Sift the flour and salt into a mixing bowl and rub in the butter with your fingertips until the mixture resembles fine breadcrumbs. Stir in the sugar and gradually work in the egg yolk and one or two tablespoons of cold water to form a soft dough. Knead the dough lightly, wrap and chill for 30 minutes.

**2** Roll out the pastry on to a lightly floured surface and use it to line a greased 23cm (9in) fluted flan tin. Prick the base and chill for a further 20 minutes.

**3** Preheat the oven to 220°C/425°F/Gas Mark 7. Line the pastry case with non-stick baking paper and baking beans and place in the oven. Bake for 10 minutes. Remove the paper and beans and bake for a further 10–12 minutes until the pastry is crisp and golden. Reduce the oven temperature to 180°C/350°F/gas mark 4.

**4** Make the filling while the pastry case is baking. In a bowl beat together the butter and sugar until pale and light and then gradually beat in the eggs, a little at a time, until incorporated. Lightly beat in all the remaining ingredients, except the pears. Pour the mixture into the pastry case.

**5** Peel and halve the pears and scoop out the cores. Thinly slice each pear lengthways without changing the shape of the pears, then use a palette knife to transfer them to the pastry case, arranging them neatly on the filling. Bake for 55–60 minutes until golden and firm in the middle. Serve warm.

# Allotment cut flowers

Ornamental cut flowers not only make the plot look more individual, they attract insects, many of which are useful for crop pollination and even control unfriendly pest insects.

## Where to grow them

There's a wide palette of plants available to create a floral paradise on the plot. Flowers can be incorporated in the vegetable garden as companion plants, and used as edging or as underplanting for fruit trees. If you just want to grow flowers to add colour to the veg plot and attract insects, your only restriction is your imagination. Plant between rows, in hanging baskets, containers, around the shed, along pathways – just about anywhere.

If you want a bed for cut flowers, choose a specific area, ideally in full sun, dig it over, enrich it with well-rotted organic matter and rake level. Growing plants in rows or blocks makes them easier to manage and look after.

## Which types

Annuals are ideal for a quick splash of colour and cost just the price of a few packs of seed. Most hardy annuals can be sown directly into the soil in spring. Others do better with a longer growing season and can be sown in autumn in a glasshouse before being hardened off and planted out in spring.

• Sow annuals in straight rows so that it is easy to tell them apart from weeds.

• Popular biennials include foxgloves, hollyhocks and wallflowers.

• Herbaceous perennials are the bedrock of the cutting garden and there are hundreds to choose from.

• Bulbous plants, including tubers, corms and rhizomes, are some of our most familiar flowers, including most of our spring flowers. But there are also lots of summer-flowering types too, such as dahlias and lilies.

## Deadheading

Keep the flowering display going for longer by removing flowerheads as they fade. This will prevent the plant directing its energy into seed production and into more flowers instead, prolonging the flowering display. It will also keep the allotment looking fresh and tidy. Most flowers should be cut or snapped off just behind the head, but some, such as delphinium, need the whole flowering stem to be cut back.

Don't deadhead flowers that you intend to collect seed from for propagating next year, and hold back on plants that produce attractive seedheads such as honesty (lunaria).

*Chrysanthemums are attractive, good for cutting for the house and draw pollinating bees and other insects.*

1. Dahlias will brighten up the plot in late summer and autumn and are an excellent cut flower.
2. Daffodils and other spring-flowering bulbs give the plot a cheery look at the beginning of the year.

*This is an excellent time to plant new fruit trees. Make sure they're planted at the same depth as they were originally growing at.*

# This month...

A few days spent on the allotment in November can pay dividends next year. OK, you'll need to wrap up warm, and a thermos of tea is an essential part of your allotment kit, but this relatively quiet time of year can be a great opportunity to undertake an autumn tidy up and reflect on the peace and quiet an allotment offers.

At this time of year, it's not necessarily the cold that you need to be concerned about, if anything it's the wet. If your soil is heavy clay, then never walk on it while it's sodden – compressing it now will drive out air and ruin the structure.

The soil is the biggest asset of your allotment, so ensure it's ready for the onset of winter by digging over vacant areas on clay soils and covering with black polythene to keep it pristine and in good condition, ready for an early start next year. Covering is especially important on light, sandy soils: autumn and winter rains can leach out nutrients, leading to poor, starving soils by spring.

And to ensure your plot is ready for growing your best crops ever next year, make sure you spend some time clearing up now. A good autumnal tidy up is more useful and therapeutic than any spring clean and will ensure you have to spend less time dealing with pest and disease problems in the future. In fact, anything you can do now will reduce the stress of next year's spring job list.

It's a great time to restock, replace or renew any fruit, especially any that's getting past its best or if there's a favourite fruit that's missing from the plot. So get planting now.

# Top veg jobs

• Sow overwintering broad beans outside (mild areas only) or plant in modules in a cold frame for planting out later. Cover with fleece or cloches to provide insulation in colder areas.

• In low rainfall areas with free-draining soil, plant garlic outdoors or plant in modules placed in a cold frame for planting out later.

• Witloof chicory crowns can be lifted for forcing to form heads (chicons) by planting up in pots in the glasshouse or cold frame. Lift the roots and discard any less than 2.5cm (1in) across at the crown. Cut back leaves to 2.5cm (1in) above the crown. Pack roots horizontally in sand in a cool shed until they are needed. Force a few at a time by planting five in a 25cm (10in) pot of moist compost, leaving the crown exposed. Cover with a black polythene bag and keep at 10–15°C (50–60°F) to produce the chicons. They are ready when 15cm (6in) high (up to four weeks).

• Stake or earth up Brussels sprout plants that look leggy and vulnerable to wind rock.

• Cover overwintering brassicas with horticultural fleece or netting to stop pigeons getting to them.

• Remove yellowed leaves from Brussels sprouts and other overwintering brassicas.

*Tie in overwintering Brussels sprouts to a sturdy stake.*

## ALLOTMENT REMINDERS

✔ Continue digging over vacant plots on clay soils.

✔ Pumpkins and winter squashes should be 'cured' in a warm place for a week or two before storing in a dry, frost-free place.

✔ Check stored vegetables, especially onions for soft rots and neck rot; *see* pages 156–7.

✔ Place mouse controls near stored fruit and vegetables.

## VEG OF THE MONTH – CHARD

Chard is easy to grow, tasty and full of goodness. Find out more on page 136.

**Chard tips:** The varieties of chard with coloured stems are the most popular, thanks to their glowing, ornamental shades. They now supersede the white-stemmed types, commonly known as Swiss chard.

• Pull off the outer leaves when they are large enough to use, and harvest regularly. Any thinnings can be used whole.

• Crops can be sown closely, scattering seeds thinly in a wide drill, and used as cut-and-come-again salad crops when leaves are 5cm (2in) long. Don't cut too close to the ground; a longer 'stump' will give the plants a better chance of sprouting again.

# November

**"Roast parsnips are a real winter treat – especially once they've been sweetened by a touch of frost"**

# Mini carrot & parsnip pies

**Serves 6**

Takes 2 hours

**Ingredients**

375g (13oz) shortcrust pastry, thawed if frozen

375g (13oz) puff pastry, thawed if frozen

1 egg, lightly beaten

**Filling**

4 tbsp olive oil

500g (1lb 2oz) button mushrooms, quartered

1 onion, finely chopped

2 garlic cloves, crushed

1 tbsp chopped thyme

250g (9oz) carrots, chopped

250g (9oz) parsnips, chopped

150ml (¼ pint) red wine

500ml (18fl oz) passata (puréed tomatoes)

salt and pepper

**1** To prepare the filling, heat half the oil in a flameproof casserole and fry the mushrooms with a little salt and pepper for 4–5 minutes until golden. Remove with a slotted spoon and set aside. Add the remaining oil to the pan and fry the onion, garlic and thyme for 5 minutes. Add the carrots and parsnips to the pan and fry for a further 5 minutes until softened and lightly golden.

**2** Pour the wine into the pan and boil rapidly for 3 minutes, then stir in the passata, mushrooms and more salt and pepper. Bring to the boil, cover and simmer for 20 minutes. Remove the lid and cook for a further 20 minutes or until the vegetables are tender and the sauce is really thick. Set aside to cool completely.

**3** Preheat the oven to 220°C/425°F/gas mark 7. Cut the shortcrust pastry into 6 equal pieces and roll them out on a lightly floured surface. Use the pastry to line 6 individual pie dishes, each 12cm (5in) across. Divide the puff pastry into 6 and roll each piece out thinly so that each piece is slightly larger than the dishes.

**4** Fill the pies with the cooled vegetable stew. Brush around the rim of the pastry with beaten egg and top with the puff pastry, pressing the edges together to seal. Trim off the excess pastry with a sharp knife and cut a small slit in the centre of each pie. Brush the tops with the beaten egg and bake for 25 minutes until golden. Serve hot.

# November

# Top fruit jobs

• November is one of the best months to plant new fruit trees, bushes and canes. Check rootstocks and pollination groups before ordering fruit trees, to ensure you get a tree that won't grow too big and any necessary pollination needs are taken into account.

• The only time you can't plant is when the ground is frozen or waterlogged.

• Make sure the soil is well prepared with plenty of added organic matter, such as well-rotted manure, compost, composted bark or tree-planting compost.

• If the planting site isn't ready when mail order plants arrive, heel in bare-root ones in a spare piece of ground to cover and protect the roots, and leave containerised ones standing outside, but water them when needed.

• Always plant at the same depth the plant was originally growing. Firm the soil around the roots.

• Trees will need to be staked with a good tree stake and secured with two tree ties.

• After planting, mulch the soil around fruit trees and bushes with a 5–7.5cm (2–3in) thick layer of organic matter to help keep weeds down and maintain soil moisture levels in summer.

*November is one of the best months to plant soft fruit.*

• Lift and divide old, unproductive crowns of rhubarb and replant in well-prepared soil with plenty of added well-rotted manure or similar bulky organic matter. Throw away any very old or rotten sections.

## ALLOTMENT REMINDERS

✔ Dig up rooted layers of blackberries and hybrid berries.

✔ Remove and destroy apples, pears and plums affected with brown rot.

✔ Do not let fallen leaves infected with diseases lie on the ground.

## FRUIT OF THE MONTH – RASPBERRIES

Raspberries are a great allotment crop, and if you don't want to bother putting up support systems for summer raspberries, grow autumn-fruiting ones.

**Raspberry tips:** Raspberries prefer a light, slightly acidic, well-drained but moisture-retentive soil. Mulch the plants each year with well-rotted manure, being careful not to apply it too deeply and smother the plant. Keep the mulch off the base of the canes or it will cause them to rot.

• Summer varieties should be trained on two parallel wires, stretched between 1.8m (6ft) posts. Prune these after fruiting.

• Plant canes in rows about 6cm (2.5in) below the soil surface. Don't plant them too deeply, or they will never grow up through the ground.

# November

"Make the most of mild
autumn weather by
restocking the plot
with new fruit trees
and bushes"

# Money-saving tricks

Having a productive plot needn't be expensive. There are lots of ways you can save money. Here's a selection of money-saving tips.

**Make your own soil improver/mulch**. Don't waste plant material – compost it. Use a good mix of ingredients, chop it up small, make your heap as big as possible (1m³/3ft³ is ideal), add some soil or nitrogen-rich fertiliser to speed up the process, and ensure it's moist but cover to exclude too much rain.

**Keep tools clean to help maintain them for longer**. Clean off soil with a scraper or wire wool then rub household oil into metal parts. Treat wooden handles with linseed oil.

**Reuse old pots, and cell and seed trays**, or pick them up cheaply or for free from your local garden centre. Wash off old compost, sterilise with bleach or Jeyes Fluid, then rinse and dry.

**Make your own pots and seed trays**. Reuse household objects, such as old food containers, such as yogurt pots, and fruit trays and punnets. Burn drainage holes with a pin or similar.

**Make your own liquid fertilisers**. Use manure or nettles for high-nitrogen feed, comfrey for high-potash or both for a balanced feed. Place in a hessian bag or pair of tights, suspend in a water butt and allow the contents to seep into the water. Dilute so that it looks like 'weak tea' for use.

**Reuse lemonade bottles**. Cut the base off and use as a mini cloche; turn upside down, fill with water and pierce two holes in the lid for a drip-watering system; or cut into rings, stick copper tape around the rim, then sink them into the ground with the tape rim above ground to protect plants against slugs and snails.

**Save seed**. Most unused vegetable seeds can be kept from year to year, providing they are kept cool, dark and dry. You can also gather seeds from your own plants to use the following year. Let seed ripen on the plant and collect it as soon as the first ones are being shed, or cut near-ripe seed heads and lay out to ripen in seed trays lined with newspaper or place in paper bags. Once the seed is ripe, store in a cool, dark place – ideally in a refrigerator or sealed, moisture-proof, labelled containers. Add moisture-holding or silica gel to keep them dry.

---

## FIVE THINGS TO DO WITH TIGHTS

1 Store onions, shallots and garlic over winter.

2 Use as tree ties.

3 Use as a 'plastic drinks cups dispenser' for a tidy way to store pots.

4 Make growing bags or flower pouches: fill the tights with compost and tie them off, then cut holes where you want the plants to go, just like normal growing bags.

5 Use as winter plant protection 'duvets': fill with mulching or insulation material and place around vulnerable plants.

---

## TEN THINGS TO KEEP AND REUSE

1 Tights (*see* above).

2 Lemonade bottles for watering aids, mini cloches and slug control (*see* left).

3 Wooden spatulas, lollipop sticks or plastic knives etc. for plant labels.

4 Newspaper for making paper pots, for use in compost heaps and bean trenches or as emergency plant protection covers.

5 Toilet rolls for sowing peas and beans.

6 Plastic coffee cups and yogurt pots for plant pots.

7 Plastic fruit trays and punnets for seedtrays.

8 Net curtains for plant protection fleece.

9 Sticks and stems for plant supports.

10 Polystyrene chips for insulation material.

# Allotment tidy up

Cleanliness is next to godliness is a good thing to remember on the allotment. Keeping the plot clean and tidy will not only help reduce pests and disease problems, but it will also keep you in your fellow plotholders' and the allotment owner's good books.

If your plot has grass paths, then make sure you keep the grass cut to a reasonable length; depending on the weather November may be the last chance before spring.

If you don't mow the grass regularly, you may get problems from any weeds seeding themselves. The grass clippings can, of course, be added to the compost heap and can even be used as a moisture-retaining mulch around some plants, such as beans, or even used in the bottom of potato trenches before planting seed potatoes.

If you don't have time for mowing, then consider replacing the grass with gravel or bark chip paths. These will be far easier to maintain.

Recut all bed edges so they look neat and tidy. This will also ensure that the grass doesn't grow into the beds, which would severely reduce yields from crops grown close to the paths.

Recover and store all the bamboo canes and other supports used through the year. Leaving them lying around not only means they're easily lost, but they will rot and can't be reused and are also a trip hazard.

## Pests and diseases

Keeping the plot clean and tidy is one of the best ways of reducing problems. Diseased leaves left lying around will provide overwintering places for disease spores, which could then spread to otherwise healthy plants. As soon as you come across diseased and discoloured leaves be sure to remove and dispose of them.

Dead leaves and yellowing leaves on overwintering crops are also best raked up and removed and, if possible, composted.

Rubbish, pruned stems and other material left on the plot are all also perfect hiding places and breeding grounds for pests, especially for slugs and snails.

Some weeds act as a secondary host for diseases, so clearing away weeds not only prevents them from competing with your crops and helps to make the plot look tidy, but also helps prevent disease problems.

Finally, digging over vacant areas will help expose overwintering pests and their eggs to cold weather and birds, which will help reduce problems next year.

*All healthy plants should be added to the compost heap to provide a great source of soil-enriching humus.*

*Recut bed edges so they look neat and tidy and prevent grasses in the paths growing into the beds.*

# Beekeeping

Bees not only provide a supply of honey, they also increase the yields of your fruit and vegetables, as they pollinate plants when they are flying from flower to flower.

## Where to keep them

Check first that you are allowed to keep bees on the allotment. If you can do so, then it's only polite to check with the people next to you on the allotment and discuss their concerns.

Honeybees are far more productive if the hive is placed in the sun. Try to place it so that the entrance is not facing onto a path or a neighbour's allotment. If you have a plot on the boundary, you can face the entrance towards the hedge or fence. If you haven't, then erect a mesh screen 2m (6½ft) high 1m (3ft) in front of the hive. This will lift the bees above head height when they are flying, ensuring that they don't collide with people.

*A smoker – a simple firebox and bellows – is used to generate smoke to subdue the bees.*

## Types of beehives

The main types used in the United Kingdom are the WBC and the National. The WBC is the traditional tiered beehive. They make a great rustic feature on the allotment, but can be harder work when inspecting bees as they have an outer skin to remove before getting to the inner boxes. The boxier Nationals are the most popular type of beehive and are easy to stack and to access the frames.

Most beehives are made of wood but there are a few new materials now available. Polystyrene hives are quickly becoming popular due to their cheapness, lightness and the extra warmth and insulation they give bees during winter. New plastic hives are also practical and easy to clean.

## Equipment

Some beekeeping equipment is not too costly: and while a honey extractor is expensive, many beekeeping associations loan them out to their members.

• Smoker: This is used to pacify the bees.

• Hive tool: This is essential for prising open the boxes.

• Protective clothing: Beginners should wear a bee suit with a veil, gloves and boots.

## Harvesting

Expect about 13.5kg (30lb) of honey from one hive in an average year, and as much as 45kg (100lb) in a good year.

Remove supers (the part of the beehive used to collect honey) from the hive in late summer and take to a bee-free shed or kitchen. Remove the capping of the honeycomb with a knife and spin frames in a centrifugal honey extractor.

The honey should be strained, allowed to settle and then bottled into jars.

A hive can contain up to 60,000 bees in the height of summer.

# DECEMBER

A cosy, warm shed may be your best friend over winter when the weather deteriorates.

# This month...

Even though 21 December is the shortest day of the year, there are still plenty of daylight hours to get out on the plot and get ahead with any necessary jobs. The shortest day does have one positive note – days will start to get longer from now on.

The end of the year is a good time to reflect. Has it been a good year, what did well, what failed? What will you grow and do again next year and what will you never do again? Did you pick the best varieties or should you try something else? Evenings spent in front of the fire, doing some armchair gardening and looking through all the fruit and vegetable catalogues, is time well spent to ensure that the following year is even more successful than this.

Drawing up a scale cropping plan on graph paper may seem excessive, but it's the best way of ensuring you buy in all the seeds you need, as well as providing a reminder for when to sow or plant out and curbing excessive enthusiasm of trying to grow more than you can physically fit into the plot.

This is the month where if you're lucky enough to have a shed you can enjoy the protection it can give from cold, wind and rain. And if your site has a communal area, then make the most of that and interrogate fellow plotholders about what worked well for them this year and which varieties produced the best results.

But don't let it be one-sided: tell them the secrets of your success, even sharing seeds of plants that did well for you, and you'll become Mr or Mrs Popular. The community aspect of allotment gardening is just one of the many good things that attracts people to this way of life.

# Top veg jobs

- Draw up your plans for next year's vegetable cropping and order seeds, and start buying canes, stakes, netting, compost, fertiliser, pesticides and everything else you'll need.

- Young broad bean plants, winter lettuce and garlic can be planted out now. Beans and lettuce will probably need cloche or fleece protection from frost, cold weather and wind.

- Plant shallots and garlic in mild areas that have well-drained soil. Garlic cloves can also be planted in modules in mild areas where the soil is less free draining.

- Thoroughly dig over any bare areas of soil, incorporating lots of well-rotted organic matter where needed and, at the same time, remove any weeds. Cover light, sandy soils with black polythene as this will prevent nutrients leaching from the soil and keep weeds down.

- Now is a good time to get ahead and prepare new asparagus beds for planting in the spring. They will need plenty of organic matter, and grit wherever drainage is a problem.

- Clean out and wash seedtrays, pots and other containers, so that they are ready for seed sowing in late winter or spring.

*Plant individual garlic cloves carefully in well-prepared soil, burying them so that only the tips are visible.*

- Lift and store root crops, such as carrots, beetroot and turnips before the weather deteriorates. Parsnips can be left in the ground until needed, or lifted and then buried in a shallow trench for easy access.

## ALLOTMENT REMINDERS

✔ Protect plants against attack from slugs.

✔ Lift and store celery or protect with straw.

✔ Jerusalem artichokes can be planted now.

## VEG OF THE MONTH – BRUSSELS SPROUTS

Even though F1s grow better, the older Brussels varieties have more flavour. For something unusual, try red varieties, such as 'Red Bull' and 'Rubine', both of which are open-pollinated.

**Sprouts tips:** Sow thinly 1cm (½in) deep in a seedbed. Thin the young seedlings to 7.5cm (3in) apart. Sow from early to mid-spring for winter to spring pickings. Early sowings may need to be covered with cloches in cold or exposed regions.

- Firm, water-retentive soil with plenty of humus is important for good crops, otherwise the sprouts 'blow', or open up.

- When the young plants are 10–15cm (4–6in) high, transplant to their growing positions 75cm (30in) apart; you can also plant short varieties 45cm (18in) apart for an earlier crop of smaller, tastier sprouts.

**"F1 hybrid Brussels sprouts are the best choice as they hold for longer and can be picked over a long period"**

# Gooseberry & elderflower fool

**Serves 4**

Takes 20 minutes, plus chilling

**Ingredients**

500g (1lb 2oz) frozen gooseberries, plus extra to decorate

3 tbsp undiluted elderflower cordial

100g (3½oz) caster sugar, plus extra to decorate

125g (4½oz) mascarpone cheese

150g (5½oz) ready-made custard

biscuits, to serve

**1** Put the frozen gooseberries in a saucepan with the cordial and sugar and cook, uncovered, for 5 minutes, stirring until softened. Transfer to a food processor or blender and blend until smooth.

**2** Add the mascarpone and custard and blend briefly until mixed. Press the mixture through a sieve, if liked, then pour the mixture into individual serving dishes. Chill for several hours.

**3** To serve decorate the tops of the fools with a few extra defrosted gooseberries rolled in a little extra sugar. Serve with dainty, crisp biscuits.

# Top fruit jobs

• Grapevines can be pruned once they're dormant; major pruning at other times can lead to severe bleeding, which will weaken the vine and may even kill it. This year's sideshoots should be hard pruned to one or two buds. Carefully rubbing off the old, loose bark of indoor vines can help deter overwintering pests.

• Start winter pruning established, freestanding apple and pear trees, but not cordons, espaliers, pyramids or fans, which should be left until summer. Pruning of all stone fruit must be left until spring or summer.

• Make sure you have a plan of attack and don't just prune for the sake of it. You should be thinking about removing the following:
a) The four Ds – this refers to any growth that is dead, dying, damaged or diseased (such as being infected by canker).
b) Growth that is crossing from one side of the tree to the other, as this can reduce airflow and increase disease problems.
c) Any branches that are rubbing, as this can damage them.
d) Any branches that are growing too low and any that are growing too tall.

• Currants and gooseberries can be pruned now. Start by thinning out very old, very thin and diseased growth.

• Prune red and white currants and gooseberries by cutting back main branches by half to three-quarters and sideshoots on these branches to one to three buds from their base.

• For black currants, cut back up to one-third to a half of all the older branches to their base to give plenty of room for young, vigorous growth. Fruit trees and bushes that are now completely dormant, have dropped all their leaves and were affected by pest problems, such as aphids, can be sprayed with a winter wash to control any overwintering eggs. Pay attention to nooks and crannies. Shoots badly affected by diseases this year are best pruned out and destroyed.

---

### ALLOTMENT REMINDERS

✔ Birds, especially bullfinches, may peck at flower buds, so give protection against birds wherever possible.

✔ Rake up leaves as they drop. Diseased leaves must be disposed of.

---

### FRUIT OF THE MONTH – GRAPES

It's easy to grow grapevines on an allotment, but unless you have a glasshouse, you'll be limited to growing wine grape varieties, as dessert grapes need more warmth.

**Grape tips:** Grapes don't need a very fertile soil; they make excessive foliage growth at the expense of fruit in such conditions. However, the soil should be improved with well-rotted manure if it is very shallow and poor.

• They need as much warmth and sun as they can get to grow and ripen the fruit. Avoid frost pockets, as a single frost in late spring will destroy emerging shoots and flowers.

• The simplest training method is to grow vertical cordons: train a single stem upwards on a post with a system of short fruiting spurs either side of it.

# December

**"**This is the time to
keep the secateurs
busy – freestanding
apples and pears,
grapevines and
gooseberries can
be pruned now**"**

# Reviewing the year

It's always interesting – and useful – to look back at the end of each year to see how the last 12 months have gone. It's all too easy to forget the details, but this year you should have an excellent record of everything you need if you filled in your weekly journal pages.

The important notes to jot down are crops grown and varieties, sowing times, weather conditions and harvest details – when each crop was ready, and whether it was a bumper yield or a disappointment.

The disappointments are usually of most interest, as there is more to learn from things that have gone wrong. If the crop is poor, this might be because you sowed it too late, didn't give the plants enough time or space to develop, sowed it too early so that it was damaged by cold weather, or it bolted to seed. Weather can play a big part; tomatoes, sweet corn and stone fruit don't like a cool, damp summer, and a drought might mean fewer runner beans and fruit.

## Which varieties?

If there is no obvious cultural reason for a poor crop, it may be that you need to try different varieties. Check through catalogues for varieties that are described as, for example, resistant to diseases or grow well in cool or hot conditions or whatever your problem was.

Some varieties, especially apples for example, are better suited to particular regional and local conditions, and these are always worth growing instead of those you're more familiar with. And, of course, fellow plotholders can provide a wealth of information: ask them which ones they grew that have done really well. Always be willing to experiment.

Finally, take into account whether you actually enjoyed the crops you grew, and whether they had a good taste, flavour and texture.

*Seeds are easily spoilt by damp; a sturdy tin with a good seal helps maintain their viability.*

*Apples can be grown in small spaces when grown on dwarf rootstocks such as M27.*

# Soft fruit

Every allotment should have an area for soft fruit. Most of the plants are compact enough to squeeze into the smallest of spaces.

## Preparing a soft fruit bed

Dig over the area, breaking up large clods of soil and removing any perennial weeds and their roots. Add plenty of well-rotted organic matter, such as manure or garden compost, rake it level and leave it to settle for a few weeks.

The method is slightly different for preparing a bed for blueberries; see page 150.

## Growing forms

Currants and gooseberries can be grown as bushes or trained into attractive ornamental shapes such as fans and cordons – or try double cordons, which make an impressive feature.

Bushes are the most common form and need no staking or wire supports. Gooseberries and red currants should be grown with an open centre, so branches growing into the centre should be removed to leave four or five main branches on a small trunk about 20cm (8in) high. Because they fruit on old wood and the base of young wood, new growth should be pruned back to two buds when the plant is dormant. The leading shoot on each branch should be cut back by one third.

Gooseberries and red currants can also be grown as standards. The training is the same as for a bush, but the central stem is much longer – about 90cm (3ft) high – so it does need a stake.

Black currants have a different growth habit and fruit on young wood produced the previous year. Because of this, they are planted deeply into the ground to encourage lots of new growth from the base each spring, known as a stool bush.

Strawberries are herbaceous plants, that can be grown in rows in a strawberry bed or as attractive features in pots, hanging baskets and growing bags.

Cane fruit includes raspberries and blackberries, including hybrids such as loganberries and tayberries. Some fruit on canes produced the previous year and should have their new shoots tied onto wires stretched between posts. Others, such as the autumn raspberries, fruit on the growth made in the current year and are simply cut down to ground level in late winter.

## Maintenance pruning

Pruning is essential to control the size of the plant and keep it in good shape.

All woody soft fruit plants should be pruned at least once a year, usually in winter. They also benefit from a second pruning in summer. This usually means cutting back some of the new growth to about five buds, thus allowing sunlight to penetrate the canopy and air to circulate around the fruit, reducing the chances of diseases. See the individual fruit of the month entries for more details.

## Netting soft fruit

When you grow soft fruit, birds will also be eyeing up the fruits of your labours. The most effective way of keeping them off your crop is to throw a net over it as soon as the fruit start to ripen. Nets may also be needed to prevent birds from pecking out the fruit buds, usually in the middle of winter.

It is possible to buy fruit frames to construct around your plants. Much cheaper, though, is building your own using bamboo canes. Place upturned pots or plastic bottles over the tops of the upright stakes to support the netting, and secure the edge to the ground using plenty of pegs or a long bar to weight it down, to prevent birds from sneaking under.

1. Blackberries look ornamental grown up a trellis.
3. After fruiting, cut down raspberries to the ground.
2. Even small strawberry plants will be productive.
4. Black currant plants produce heavy summer crops.

# Resources

## USEFUL ORGANISATIONS

**Garden Organic**
Ryton Organic Garden
Coventry, Warwickshire
CV8 3LG
Tel: 024 7630 3517
www.gardenorganic.org.uk
Garden Organic (previously
known as the Henry Doubleday
Research Association) is an
organic growing charity
dedicated to researching and
promoting organic gardening,
farming and food.

**National Society of Allotment
and Leisure Gardeners**
O'Dell House
Hunters Road, Corby
Northants NN17 5JE
Tel: 01536 266576
www.nsalg.org.uk
The aims of the society are to
protect, promote and preserve
allotment gardening, and to help
all to enjoy the pleasures of
allotment and leisure gardening.

**National Vegetable Society**
5 Whitelow Road
Heaton Moor, Stockport
SK4 4BY
www.nvsuk.org.uk
Charity dedicated to advancing
the culture, study and
improvement of vegetables,
offering help and advice to
novice and expert show-
grower alike.

**Royal Horticultural Society**
80 Vincent Square
London
SW1P 2PE
Tel: 0845 260 5000
www.rhs.org.uk
Gardening charity dedicated
to advancing horticulture and
promoting good gardening.

## VEGETABLE SEED SUPPLIERS

**D T Brown & Co**
Bury Road
Kentford, Newmarket
Suffolk CB8 7PR
Tel: 0845 166 2275
www.dtbrownseeds.co.uk

**Samuel Dobie & Son**
Long Road
Paignton, Devon
TQ4 7SX
Tel: 0844 701 7623
www.dobies.co.uk

**Kings Seeds**
Monks Farm
Kelvedon, Colchester
Essex
CO5 9PG
Tel: 01376 570000
www.kingsseeds.com

**S E Marshall & Co**
Alconbury Hill
Huntingdon, Cambs
PE28 4HY
Tel: 01480 443390
www.marshalls-seeds.co.uk

**Mr Fothergill's**
Gazeley Road
Kentford, Newmarket
Suffolk
CB8 7QB
Tel: 0845 371 0518
www.mr-fothergills.co.uk

**Nicky's Nursery**
Fairfield Road
Broadstairs, Kent
CT10 2JU
Tel: 01843 600972
www.nickys-nursery.co.uk

**Organic Gardening Catalogue**
Riverdene Business Park
Molesey Road
Hersham, Surrey
KT12 4RG
Tel: 01932 253 666
www.organiccatalog.com

**The Real Seed Catalogue**
VidaVerde
Brithdir Mawr Farm
Newport near Fishguard
Pembrokeshire
SA42 0QJ
Tel: 01239 821107
www.vidaverde.co.uk

**Robinson's Mammoth
Vegetable Seeds**
Sunny Bank
Forton near Preston
Lancs
PR3 0BN
Tel: 01524 791210
www.mammothonion.co.uk

**Seeds of Italy**
C3 Phoenix Industrial Estate
Rosslyn Crescent
Harrow
Middlesex
HA1 2SP
Tel: 020 8427 5020
www.seedsofitaly.com

**Simpson's Seeds**
The Walled Garden Nursery
Horningsham
Warminster
Somerset
BA12 7NQ
Tel: 01985 845004
www.simpsonsseeds.co.uk

**Suttons Seeds**
Woodview Road
Paignton
Devon
TQ4 7NG
Tel: 0844 922 2899
www.suttons-seeds.co.uk

**Tamar Organics**
Cartha Martha Farm
Rezare
Launceston
Cornwall
PL15 9NX
Tel: 01579 371087
www.tamarorganics.co.uk

**Thompson & Morgan (UK)**
Poplar Lane
Ipswich
Suffolk
IP8 3BU
Tel: 0844 248 5383
www.thompson-morgan.com

**Edwin Tucker & Sons**
Brewery Meadow
Stonepark
Ashburton
Newton Abbot
Devon TQ13 7DG
Tel: 01364 652233
www.edwintucker.com

**Unwins Seeds**
Alconbury Hill
Huntingdon
Cambs
PE28 4HY
Tel: 01480 443395
www.unwins.co.uk

## EQUIPMENT SUPPLIERS

**Agralan**
The Old Brickyard
Ashton Keynes
Swindon
Wilts
SN6 6QR
Tel: 01285 860015
www.agralan.co.uk
Wide range of products,
including horticultural fleece
and plant protection mesh,
cloches and biological controls.

**Agriframes**
Hartcliffe Way
Bristol
BS3 5RJ
Tel: 0845 260 4450
www.agriframes.co.uk
Fruit cages, plant supports,
fleece, cloches, watering
equipment etc.

**Crocus.co.uk**
Nursery Court
London Road
Windlesham, Surrey
GU20 6LQ
Tel: 0844 557 2233
www.crocus.co.uk
Online supplier of vegetable
plants and seeds, cold
frames, cloches, garden
tools and equipment.

**Ferndale Lodge**
Woodview Road
Paignton, Devon
TQ4 7NG
Tel: 0844 314 1342
www.ferndale-lodge.co.uk
Wide range of products for the
vegetable garden, including
polytunnels, pots and trays,
tools, raised beds, netting,
hessian sacks, fruit cages
and cloches.

**Garden Warehouse**
Standroyd Mill
Cottontree
Colne
Lancs
BB8 7BW
Tel: 01282 873370
www.lbsgardenwarehouse.co.uk
Wide range of gardening items,
including fencing and netting,
watering equipment, plant
supports, biological controls,
organic products, composts,
fertilisers, tools and fruit cages.

**Green Gardener**
Chandlers End
Mill Road
Stokesby
Great Yarmouth
Norfolk
NR29 3EY
Tel: 01493 750 061
www.greengardener.co.uk
Specialists in biological
controls, plus stockists of a
wide range of environmentally
friendly gardening products.

**Harrod Horticultural**
Pinbush Road
Lowestoft
Suffolk
NR33 7NL
Tel: 0845 402 5300
www.harrodhorticultural.com
Wide range of products, including
raised beds, fruit cages, netting,
organic seeds and fertilisers,
biological pest control, vegetable
storage racks and trusses.

**Haxnicks**
Beaumont Business Centre
Woodlands Road
Mere
Wiltshire
BA12 6BT
Tel: 01747 861539
www.haxnicks.co.uk
Wide range of gardening
products, including fleece,
cloches, tunnels, tools and
raised beds.

**Two Wests and Elliott**
Unit 4
Carrwood Road
Sheepbridge Industrial Estate
Chesterfield
Derbyshire
S41 9RH
Tel: 01246 451077
www.twowests.co.uk
Wide range of gardening
products, including glasshouse
sundries, cloches, tunnels,
frames, propagators and
watering equipment.

# Glossary

**ACID SOIL** Soil with a pH measurement of below 7 containing no lime or only small amounts of lime. Certain plants such as blueberries are sensitive to lime and will only grow in acid soils.

**AGM** The Award of Garden Merit is awarded by the Royal Horticultural Society to plants that are judged to be of outstanding all-round excellence.

**ALKALINE SOIL** Soil with a pH measurement of above 7 containing some lime.

**ANNUAL** A plant that completes its life cycle in one season.

**BARE-ROOT** Refers to plants that have been grown in a field, then lifted and sold without being potted into a container.

**BIOLOGICAL CONTROL** The use of the natural enemies of pests and diseases to control them, instead of chemicals.

**BLOSSOM END ROT** A disorder causing a shrivelled, blackened area to develop at the base of tomatoes and peppers that have not received enough water while the fruits were forming.

**BOLTING** The premature production of flowers and seed which, in the case of lettuces, for example, makes the leaves taste bitter.

**BRASSICA** A plant belonging to the cabbage family.

**CATCH CROP** A quick-maturing crop for growing between the harvesting of one crop and the growing of the next.

**CHITTING** Allowing potato tubers to form sprouts before planting, usually to ensure an earlier crop.

**CLAY** Soil composed of very small particles, which is prone to waterlogging, difficult to dig and slow to warm up in spring.

**CLOCHE** A low glass or plastic covering used to protect young plants from adverse weather conditions early or late in the year.

**COMPOST** Garden compost is the decomposed remains of garden waste used as a soil conditioner. Compost is a proprietary bagged growing medium for plants in containers.

**CONTAINERISED** Referring to a plant that has been potted up into a container.

**CONTROLLED-RELEASE** Describes a fertiliser that releases its nutrients gradually over an extended period of time, according to temperature and soil moisture.

**CORDON** Plant trained to a single stem.

**CROWN** The base of a plant where stem and roots join.

**DAMPING OFF** Fungal disease that destroys emerging seedlings by rotting the stems at soil level.

**DIBBER** Pointed tool used for making holes in soil, ready to receive plants or seedlings.

**DRILL** Shallow groove or furrow made in the soil for sowing seed.

**EARTHING UP** Drawing up soil around a plant – potatoes, for example – to stop the tubers turning green, or leeks to keep the stems white. Also to help anchor some plants in the ground and stop them rocking in the wind.

**ERICACEOUS** Describing lime-free or acid soil, or a plant that grows in such soil.

**ESPALIER** A fruit tree with a vertical trunk from which side branches are trained vertically either side.

**F1 HYBRID** Plants or seeds that have been bred under strict conditions to create a crop that is uniform, vigorous and high yielding. Seeds gathered from F1 hybrids will not come true to type, so you will need to buy fresh stock for the next year.

**FLEECE** A lightweight, finely woven material laid over crops to protect them against pests or cold weather.

**FORCING** Growing plants in protected conditions to produce earlier or more tender growth.

**GREEN MANURE** Plants that are grown specifically to be dug into the soil to improve its structure and fertility.

**GROWING BAG** A plastic sack of compost intended to be planted directly with vegetables, such as tomatoes, usually in a glasshouse or on a patio.

**HARDENING OFF** The process of acclimatising tender or half-hardy plants raised with warmth indoors to outdoor conditions by gradual exposure to lower temperatures.

**HAULM** The top growth of crops such as potatoes and peas.

**HEEL IN** To cover the roots and bases of plants with a shallow layer of soil to prevent them from drying out.

**HUMUS** Decomposed organic matter in the soil, which improves its water-holding capacity and structure.

**INTERCROPPING** Growing a quick maturing crop between slower growing ones.

**JOHN INNES COMPOST** A loam-based compost produced to a standard recipe developed by the John Innes Institute in the 1930s.

**JUNE DROP** The seasonal natural dropping of immature fruitlets from fruit trees.

**LATERAL SHOOT** A sideshoot.

**LOAM** A fertile soil that consists of a mixture of clay, sand and organic matter (humus).

**MODULE** An arrangement of small, individual plastic plant pots joined together to fit in a seedtray.

**MULCH** A thick covering over the soil, usually of well-rotted compost or similar. Its many advantages include locking moisture in the ground by reducing evaporation; insulating the roots of plants in cold winters; blocking out weeds; and improving soil structure.

**NEMATODES** Small, soil-living, worm-like creatures, some of which cause disease, while others are useful as biological control agents.

**OFFSET** Young plant attached to the parent, which can be separated and grown on.

**OPEN POLLINATED** Plants that are pollinated without special control – in other words, producing non-hybrid seeds.

**ORGANIC GARDENING** A method of growing plants and promoting soil fertility by natural means, without manufactured chemicals such as insecticides and herbicides.

**ORGANIC MATTER** Matter derived from anything that has once lived – for example, garden compost produced from plant remains. Plays a valuable part in improving soil structure.

**PERENNIAL** Plant living for more than two years.

**PERPETUAL** Plant, such as strawberry, with a long flowering and fruiting period, in bloom more or less continuously.

**pH** A scale used to measure acidity or alkalinity. *See* Acid/Alkaline soil.

**PINCH OUT** Remove the growing tip by nipping it off with finger and thumb, encouraging the growth of sideshoots.

**POTAGER** An ornamental kitchen garden, mixing flowers and produce.

**POTASH** Another name for potassium, a nutrient that improves the flowering and fruiting of plants.

**POTTING COMPOST** Proprietary compost that has been produced for potting up plants after the seedling stage, containing more nutrients than sowing compost.

**PRIMOCANES** A method of producing raspberry canes that fruit in their first year.

**PROPAGATOR** A usually heated, glass or plastic covered box-like structure for raising seedlings or cuttings.

**RHIZOME** A spreading underground stem that looks like a root. Weeds with rhizomes, such as couch grass, are difficult to control as any small piece of rhizome broken off and left in the soil will produce a new plant.

**ROOTSTOCK** The lower part of the trunk and the root system of a fruit tree onto which a fruiting variety is grafted.

**ROTATION** Growing annual vegetables in different sites each year, primarily carried out to prevent the build-up of pests and diseases and to maintain nutrients in the soil.

**RUNNER** A slender stem extending from a plant on the surface of the ground and producing roots and small plants, as in strawberries.

**SEED, RUNNING TO** *See* Bolting.

**SEED POTATO** A potato tuber that is allowed to develop shoots before being planted and growing into a new plant. 'Certified' seed potatoes are guaranteed to be free of pests and disease when supplied for planting.

**SEEDBED** A specially prepared area of the garden that has been prepared for seed sowing, the soil broken down into very fine crumbs or particles and raked level to promote germination.

**SIDESHOOT** A lateral growth.

**SOWING AND CUTTING COMPOST** Proprietary compost formulated for seed sowing and the rooting of cuttings. It has lower levels of nutrients than potting compost.

**STOOL BUSH** A method of growing fruit, such as black currants, where the main stem is cut down to promote new growth.

**SUCCESSIONAL SOWING** Making small sowings at regular intervals to ensure a continuous supply of a crop and avoid one big glut.

**TASSELS** The silky, thread-like male flowers of sweetcorn, which carry pollen to fertilise the female flowers, so producing corn kernels.

**TENDER** Describing plants that are damaged by cold temperatures.

**THINNING** Removing some seedlings or plants to make sure that those left are evenly spaced with enough room to grow and can access adequate light and food supplies.

**TOP GROWTH** The parts of a plant above ground.

**TOPSOIL** The top layer of fertile soil in which plants' roots grow.

**TRANSPLANT** To move a seedling or plant from one place to another; for example, a tender seedling from a small to a larger pot or out into the garden. Also (noun) a plant being so moved.

**TRUSS** A stem carrying a number of regularly spaced flowers or fruits, such as is found on a tomato plant.

**TUBER** An underground storage organ of a plant, for example a potato or Jerusalem artichoke.

**WILT** The collapse of a plant, caused by fungal disease or lack of water.

# Conversion charts

| TEMPERATURE | | LENGTH | | WEIGHT | | FLUIDS | |
|---|---|---|---|---|---|---|---|
| -20°C | -4°F | 3mm | ⅛in | 5g | ⅛oz | 5ml | ⅛fl oz |
| -15°C | 5°F | 5mm | ¼in | 10g | ¼oz | 10ml | ¼fl oz |
| -10°C | 14°F | 1cm | ½in | 15g | ½oz | 15ml | ½fl oz |
| -5°C | 23°F | 2cm | ¾in | 30g | 1oz | 20ml | ¾fl oz |
| 0°C | 32°F | 2.5cm | 1in | 35g | 1¼oz | 30ml | 1fl oz |
| 1°C | 34°F | 3cm | 1¼in | 40g | 1½oz | 50ml | 2fl oz |
| 2°C | 36°F | 4cm | 1½in | 50g | 1¾oz | 75ml | 2½fl oz |
| 3°C | 37°F | 4.5cm | 1¾in | 60g | 2¼oz | 100ml | 3½fl oz |
| 4°C | 39°F | 5cm | 2in | 70g | 2½oz | 125ml | 4fl oz |
| 5°C | 41°F | 7cm | 2½in | 85g | 3oz | 150ml | 5fl oz |
| 6°C | 43°F | 7.5cm | 3in | 90g | 3¼oz | 175ml | 6fl oz |
| 7°C | 45°F | 8cm | 3½in | 100g | 3½oz | 200ml | 7fl oz |
| 8°C | 46°F | 10cm | 4in | 200g | 7oz | 225ml | 8fl oz |
| 9°C | 48°F | 12cm | 5in | 225g | 8oz | 250ml | 9fl oz |
| 10°C | 50°F | 15cm | 6in | 300g | 10½oz | 300ml | 10fl oz |
| 11°C | 52°F | 18cm | 7in | 400g | 14oz | 400ml | 14fl oz |
| 12°C | 54°F | 20cm | 8in | 450g | 1lb | 500ml | 18fl oz |
| 13°C | 55°F | 23cm | 9in | 500g | 1lb 2oz | 568ml | 1pt |
| 15°C | 59°F | 25cm | 10in | 650g | 1lb 7oz | 1l | 1¾pt |
| 16°C | 61°F | 27cm | 11in | 700g | 1lb 9oz | 2l | 3½pt |
| 17°C | 63°F | 30cm | 12in | 800g | 1lb 12oz | 2.5l | 4½pt |
| 18°C | 64°F | 50cm | 20in | 900g | 2lb | 3l | 5¼pt |
| 19°C | 66°F | 75cm | 30in | 1kg | 2lb 4oz | 4.5l | 8pt/1gal |
| 20°C | 68°F | 80cm | 2½ft | 1.5kg | 3lb 5oz | 5l | 9pt |
| 21°C | 70°F | 1m | 3ft | 2kg | 4lb 8oz | 6l | 10½pt |
| 22°C | 72°F | 1.1m | 3½ft | 2.25kg | 5lb | 7l | 12¼pt |
| 23°C | 73°F | 1.2m | 4ft | 2.7kg | 6lb | 8l | 14pt |
| 24°C | 75°F | 1.5m | 5ft | 3kg | 6lb 8oz | 9l | 15¾pt |
| 25°C | 77°F | 1.75m | 5½ft | 4.5kg | 10lb | 10l | 2¼gal |
| 26°C | 79°F | 2m | 6½ft | 5kg | 11lb | 20l | 4½gal |
| 27°C | 80°F | 2.5m | 8ft | 6kg | 13lb 3oz | 22.5l | 5gal |
| 28°C | 82°F | 3m | 10ft | 7kg | 15lb 7oz | 30l | 6½gal |
| 29°C | 85°F | 5m | 16ft | 8kg | 17lb 10oz | 40l | 8¾gal |
| 32°C | 90°F | 10m | 33ft | 9kg | 20lb | 45.5l | 10gal |
| 60°C | 140°F | 20m | 66ft | 10kg | 22lb | 50l | 11gal |

## CONVERSION FACTORS

**TO CONVERT:**
**g to oz** multiply by 0.035
**oz to g** multiply by 28.349

**kg to lb** multiply by 2.205
**lb to kg** multiply by 0.454

**g per sq m to oz per sq yd** multiply by 0.0295
**oz per sq yd to g per sq m** divide by 33.91

**mm to in** multiply by 0.0394
**in to mm** multiply by 25.4

**cm to in** multiply by 0.394
**in to cm** multiply by 2.54

**cm³ to in³** multiply by 0.061
**in³ to cm³** multiply by 16.387

**litre to pint** multiply by 1.76
**pint to litre** multiply by 0.568

**litre to gallon** multiply by 0.22
**gallon to litre** multiply by 4.546

**m³ to ft³** multiply by 35.315
**ft³ to m³** multiply by 0.028

# Index

# Picture credits

All photographs are by Jo Whitworth for Octopus Publishing Group with the exception of the following:

**Alamy** FoodCollection.com 140, 194;

**Corbis** ImageSource 5 below right, 105 below left, 190; Mark Bolton 188; Markus Botzek 103 below; Peter Frank 173;

**Fotolia** .shock 104; Andrzej W£#322;odarczyk 132 below; ason 76; audaxl 67; Bluestock 121, 126 above right; Calek 144 below left; chiyacat 148; Chris Leachman 60; claireliz 134; Clivia 16 right; Colette 5 below left; Dario Sabljak 23; Denis Dryashkin 12 left; Douglas Gingerich 78; Elena Moiseeva 56 below; Elena Schweitzer 164; Elenathewise 68; Hazel Proudlove 5 above right, 38; Heinrich 24; Inspir8tion 65 above right; Kadmy 65 above left; karnizz 64; kaz 72; komandos 102; Lulu 69; Margo Harrison 65 below right, 146 below; Maria Brzostowska 46; MarkFGD 152; mirrormere 12 right; Monika Adamczyk 112; Nadezda Verbenko 145 above right; Neil Chillingworth 171 below; Norman Chan 170; Olga Lyubkina 42 above; Oleg Fedorkin 122; Olga D van de Veer 103 above; Oriental Trade 5 above left; Patrick Hermans 137 above right; PaulPaladin 168; Picture Partners 178; Vaida 33; Sally Wallis 96; siloto 150 below; Witold Krasowski 157 above left; Zee 80 below; Ziablik 26;

**GAP Photos** FhF Greenmedia 86; Juliette Wade 52, 74; Lynn Keddie 47; Mark Bolton 6, 20, 34;

**Octopus Publishing Group** Jane Sebire 16 left, 192 above; Mark Winwood 62 above; Torie Chugg 14, 22 above left and right, 28 above, 30, 32, 44 above, 98 above, 108 above right, 114 above and below, 117, 132 above, 157 above right, 158, 174, 180 above, 201 above left and below left;

**RHS Herbarium** Graham Titchmarsh 44 below.